MEN *Sharpen* MEN

Messages For Inspiration and Meditation for Men

IAN WILSON

MEN *Sharpen* MEN
Messages For Inspiration and Meditation for Men
Copyright © 2023 Ian Wilson

All rights reserved.

Although the author has made every effort to ensure that the information in this book was correct at press time, the author does not assume and hereby disclaim any liability to any party for any loss, damage, or disruption caused by errors or omissions, whether such errors or omissions result from negligence, accident, or any other cause.

No parts of this book may be reproduced in any form or by any electronic or mechanical means, including information storage in retrieval systems, without written permission from the author, except in the case of a reviewer, who may quote brief passages embodied in critical articles or in a review.

All scripture references used in this book were taken from the Holy Bible, New International Version and can be found at http://thebiblegateway.com.

Paperback ISBN: 979-8-9883457-5-6
Hardcover ISBN: 979-8-9883457-9-4

Editor: Crystal S. Wright

10 9 8 7 6 5 4 3 2 1

Printed in the United States

DEDICATION

*To the Almighty God, my Creator,
who is the inspiration of this book...*

*Thank you for giving me this dream
and the resources to bring it to fruition.*

*To my loving wife, Caroll,
and our family...*

*Thank you for your love, unwavering support,
and encouragement.*

⟵——————⟶

MEDITATE on these *Messages*,
so you can use them to **INSPIRE** you.

⟵——————⟶

ACKNOWLEDGEMENTS

I believe that God sometimes challenges us to test how good a friend we are. He puts circumstances before us that requires that we sacrifice our comfort, time, or resources.

I remember when someone close to me was experiencing financial hardship and needed some help coming up with rent. I was willing to come through with a portion but a bit more would ease her pain significantly. So, I began to think of who I could approach to help out. This wasn't a piece of cake for me because I dreaded the possibility of rejection and embarrassment that welled up in my mind. I also had to make sure my selection was a person not lacking in discretion or integrity. It must not be someone who would put this woman's business in the streets. He also had to have some cash to spare. After my bout of brain wracking, the only person I felt comfortable and confident to approach, was our (the beneficiary and mine) mutual friend Clarence.

The man didn't blink an eye or interrogate me about the situation. His coming forth with help seemed so effortless. The way I remembered it, it was his assistance that enabled each of us to pay one month's rent. That made an indelible impact on me.

I initially kept the writing of this book to myself, declining to share it with even the closest people to me. What for some might be a pedestrian pursuit, was for me a nervous one. Writing this book made me vulnerable. Though I knew I had the ability, there was still a feeling of inadequacy. Who was I to write a book of inspiration and meditations?

But when I completed the first draft, I had to find people to read it through and give feedback. To whom could I entrust this secret project? I reached out to my old friend, **Clarence**, himself now a published author. He read and proofread the manuscript, providing comments and corrections. Thank you, Clarence.

On my way home one afternoon, I called on my oldest friend, **Reggie**. I told him about the project and asked him to take a look at it as a personal favor. A few days passed and I called him, with some trepidation, to find out if he had read the book. A very satisfying rush of joy went through me when he told me he had, and that he loved it. Not only that, he had started to use the rough draft of the manuscript for daily meditation. Thank you, Reggie.

I also called on my friend, **Lenny**, who has always supported me morally and spiritually. I was very appreciative of how quickly he read the manuscript. It was Lenny who suggested that I include scriptures. Thank you, Lenny.

I had to get a woman's perspective on the material so I sent it to my friend, **Niecey**. I am thankful to her for recommending that I place a subject line before each meditation. This helped the material flow better than the way I had structured it originally. Thank you, Niecey.

Finally, I would like to acknowledge the support of my friend, **Miranda Gardner**, who despite having a hectic grad school schedule, made time to read and review my work. Thank you, Miranda.

I am eternally grateful to God for blessing me with these people. Despite my fears, their encouragement and support were instrumental to the completion of the book in your hands today. The investment of their time was not just a personal favor to me. I believe they saw and acknowledged the value that the content within this book could bring to men who read them.

This is my prayer: that this book will bring value to the lives of men, and to the lives of the people around them.

In gratitude,
Ian

INTRODUCTION

I never saw myself as a writer or even an artist. I always doubted that I had any special gifts, much less one that would make me able to create a narrative or pen words from my very own imagination. However, having reflected on the experiences that I have had throughout my life and the lessons I've gathered, I felt I had something to share and a point of view. These experiences have informed my character and convictions and shaped the principles by which I live and love.

My personal journey has been both painful and joyful. Pain was often the result of me trying to navigate a world for which I had no instruction manual. The joyful part came about when I discovered that I was being influenced and helped by other men who were placed in my path. These men would provide love, support, encouragement, and guidance. They acknowledged and understood my pain, anger, fears, and insecurities.

They told me the unvarnished truth about myself, whether I wanted to hear it or not. My brothers bared their souls to me, validating my feelings and letting me know that I was not unique, different or alone. They exposed their scars, lessons, and mistakes so that I could learn from them and have a blueprint for helping others. I could not have made it without these men.

The changes I've experienced in my life that were made possible only by the grace of God operating through other men, have made me realize that I am not unique. There are many men who are facing the challenges that accompany the human existence.

Giving of my self on these pages is my way of expressing my gratitude and paying it forward.

In the process of compiling and documenting these inspirational messages, I experienced somewhat of a shift in my own mindset. I started out thinking about how I could make this book appealing to a broad market. To accomplish that, my aim was to limit, if not exclude altogether, any talk of God. That would make it attractive to a wide audience, I thought. However, the God I tried to suppress had other plans for me.

When my friend, Lenny, suggested that the addition of a relevant scripture verse would add value for the reader, I resisted at first. His suggestion countered the vision I had for the branding of the book. My thinking was that adding scriptures would make the book undoubtedly Christian, thus making it less marketable.

I began to examine Lenny's idea through the lens of my core values. Who should get the glory for bringing this project to life? In record time, I came to see that this book should not be about me. For it to bring true value to you, my reader, God has to be at the center of it all. After all, God knows you intimately and He knows what you need — I do not.

Also, who am I that my words should hold weight to you? The words of our Creator should be the highest authority in our lives. With this in mind, I added scripture that further illuminate each meditation. I hope these verses find their way to your heart, as they have to mine. Though I have only included one verse per entry, if you feel led to read multiple verses or even an entire chapter of scripture, go ahead.

It's said that what comes from the heart, reaches the heart. My hope is that you are assured that the ideas I share come from a place of love and humility. My other wish is that you will use this book as a tool in your quest for a life of peace and contentment.

Ideally, I would like you to use this book as a daily companion. I've tried to be as simple and practical as possible. I pray that you will approach each topic with an open mind, and the courage to reflect on what it means to you. After reflecting, I pray you will be willing to put into practice whatever applies to you.

Prayerfully, my words will uplift, comfort, challenge, and inspire you.

> **"...give thanks in all circumstances...."**
> – 1 Thessalonians 5:16-18

TODAY AND EVERY DAY, LET'S THANK GOD.

Thank you, Lord. Thank you for bringing me this far. Thank you for bringing me through all the trials, all the adversities, and all the anxieties. Thank you for all my blessings. Thank you for all that you have given me, all that You have left me and all that You have taken from me. Thank You for protecting me even when I didn't know You were doing it. Thank You for keeping me. Thank You for loving me. I thank You that I know that You are the one to thank. Lord God, I thank You.

> **"FOR WHERE YOUR TREASURE IS, THERE YOUR HEART WILL BE ALSO."**
> — Matthew 6:21

TODAY I WILL EXAMINE WHICH ONE I'M GIVING MORE ATTENTION — MY PERSON OR MY PROFESSION.

TODAY AND EVERY DAY I COMMIT TO WORKING ON ME MORE THAN ANYTHING ELSE.

Because many of us prioritize the acquisition of financial and material wealth over personal growth, we sometimes wind up with a mind full of regrets for the things we neglected such as family and friends. There is absolutely nothing wrong with the pursuit of professional excellence. However, the perfection of our person must be placed, if even slightly, ahead of the perfection of our profession. The investment of time and energy in our own personal growth, and the development of the relationships with family and friends will pay huge dividends. When we invest in our personal growth, we are almost guaranteed to succeed in our profession. But if we place our profession before all else, it's likely we will neglect other aspects of our life and wind up regretting we did.

> **Whoever walks in integrity walks securely,
> but whoever takes crooked paths will be found out.**
> - Proverbs 10:9

TODAY, LET'S LOOK AT HOW WE GO INTO OUR RELATIONSHIPS.

Have you ever noticed that most of the regrets we have come at the end of a relationship, rather than the beginning? How could such a hopeful and happy beginning be followed by such a painful and disastrous end? The exciting romance becomes bitter. The love of our life seemingly transforms into someone out of a nightmare. The dream job that we were so enthusiastic about turns out to be a curse. We can all relate to having at least one such experience. I fear that for some of us, it has become a cycle. Why, do things end the same way all the time? To break this pattern of unhappy endings, we must reflect on our beginnings. How are we getting into relationships and situations? Do we move too fast and too soon? Are our motives bad? Did you give it your best effort? Do we reflect on each situation before moving into a new one? Do we apply the lessons or repeat the mistakes? Be brutally honest with yourself. What part have you played in the disappointment and unhappy endings? Shift your focus from the ending and look at the beginning. What you might find is that you have been repeating an error from the start that has ensured a similar outcome. So, the end was already established at the start. What changes can you make to stop this pattern from continuing?

> "What then shall we say about these things? If God be for us, who can be against us."
> – Romans 8:31

TODAY, I CAN FEEL GOOD ABOUT MY EFFORTS AND GIVE MYSELF CREDIT FOR TRYING TO DO MY BEST.

I WON'T LET PEOPLE'S EXPECTATION OR THAT *LITTLE VOICE* DISCOURAGE ME.

Have you ever heard a little voice in your head whispering, "You're not good enough? You could've done better. You should've known better. You're failing. You didn't work hard enough. You quit too soon, gave up too quickly. What's wrong with you?" What does the negative voice say to you? That negative voice can be quite disturbing and depressing. The criticism that comes from it can be painful and discouraging. On top of that inner critic, you have people in your life who demand your presence and performance. You may have parents, siblings, a partner, friend or other loved one who is seemingly always dissatisfied with you and demanding more. One thing I have learned is that we cannot control others. Let people say what they like and believe what they want to. Show up each day and give your best effort. When you falter, as we all do, give yourself grace. You know how hard you're trying and what's more, God knows too. And that's good enough.

> "Let your eyes look directly forward, and your gaze be straight before you."
> – Proverbs 4:25

TODAY, THINK ABOUT AT LEAST ONE THING YOU WANT TO ACQUIRE OR ACCOMPLISH, A PLACE YOU WANT TO VISIT, OR A CHANGE YOU WANT TO MAKE.

START MOVING FORWARD RIGHT NOW, FROM RIGHT WHERE YOU ARE.

There's a story told about a lost traveler who stopped at an old farmhouse to get directions to his destination. After listening to the traveler's situation, the farmer said to the traveler, *"Well, you can't really get there from here. You got to start over on the other side of the mountains..."* The farmer was dead wrong. The only way to get anywhere is to start from right where you are. If we are honest, we will see that we are much like the old farmer. How often have you said, *"When I get a large sum of money, I'll start saving,"* or *"When I lose 15 pounds, I'll start exercising"* or *"When my kids are grown, I'll start traveling."* If the start of your journey toward a dream or destination is contingent on a variable you cannot control, you will never attain it. You have today. Start now.

> "Be completely humble and gentle; be patient, bearing with one another in love."
>
> – Ephesians 4:2

TODAY, LET'S EXAMINE OUR INTIMATE RELATIONSHIPS. HAVE WE BEEN TAKING THE EASY WAY OUT?

HAVE WE BEEN PUTTING SEX AHEAD OF A MEANINGFUL, PERSONAL CONNECTION?

This might burst a lot of people's bubble, but it takes very little brainpower to have sex. How high an IQ do you need to implement an up and down or in and out motion with your pelvis? Sex is that easy. Maybe that's why we attach such great importance to it. It is easy. Aren't we inclined to opt for things that promise pleasure and low effort? Relationships, on the other hand, require courage, commitment, communication skills, vulnerability, and time. Relationships aren't easy, but when done right, they are totally worth it.

> "Do not withhold good from those to whom it is due, when it is in your power to do it."
> - Proverbs 3:27

TODAY, LET'S DECIDE TO LOVE PEOPLE TO THE BEST OF OUR ABILITY, EVEN THOSE WE DON'T LIKE.

LET'S PUT FEELINGS ASIDE AND LOVE THEM ANYWAY.

Today is a day like any other. Each day, we are bound to meet people we like and some that we don't. There will be undoubtedly people who annoy us and get on our last nerve. The question is, how will we respond? How do you relate to those people who are difficult to like, much less love? Love them anyway. Surely, there are some who may find you difficult to handle. Wouldn't you hope that they choose to treat you well? Love is not just a feeling. It's an action that starts with the decision to love. It's a conscious and intentional decision to act in the best interest of the other person. Truth is, you don't have to like anyone. What we can do is give them the respect we would want for ourselves. Today, try to be patient and kind regardless of how you feel about the person.

> "There is a way that seems right to a man, but its end is the way to death."
> – Proverbs 14:12

TODAY I WILL THINK ABOUT HOW I'M LIVING MY LIFE.

TODAY I WILL THINK ABOUT THE KIND OF LIFE I WANT FOR MYSELF.

A lot of people live their lives running after good food and drink, recreation, fine clothes and entertainment. They measure the quality of their lives by the presence or absence of these things. In reality, "good-time" living is shallow and unfulfilling. The person who lives primarily for good times is happy only when times are good and when they're having fun. The thing is, when we make good times the priority of our lives, we may fail to have a good life. What is the "good" life? The good life is what the "good time" life is not. The good life is not debt-ridden, anxiety-laden, strife-filled, bitter, angry, or shame-based. The good life may not be free from problems, trouble and adversity. However, when bad things come into your "good life", they will help you grow and make your good life even better. Remember, it's your choice — the good life or good times. If you choose the good life, you're guaranteed to have good times. If you choose to prioritize good times, it's almost guaranteed, you won't have a good life.

> **"Cast all your anxiety on Him because he cares for you."**
> – 1 Peter 5:7

TONIGHT, IF YOU CAN'T SLEEP, THERE MIGHT BE A GOOD REASON FOR IT.

MAKE THE BEST USE OF YOUR TIME AWAKE. DO SOME GOOD THINKING.

No one likes a sleepless night. When we have difficulty falling asleep or our rest is interrupted, we associate our insomnia with some negative feeling, emotions, or incident. But, there is a positive side to this. The night can be a good time to do some serious thinking. That period of time before sleep comes, can be used for reflection and seeking solutions to problems you may be facing. The quiet of the night allows us to hear our thoughts, questions, and the answers we receive. While the rest of our household and the world sleep, we can be praying, planning, strategizing, analyzing, dreaming, meditating, composing, creating, writing, rehearsing or reminiscing. So, when the next sleepless night comes, make it work for you. Remember, the night wasn't made only for sleeping. It was also made for thinking.

> **"Thanks be to God for His inexpressible gift."**
> - 2 Corinthians 9:15

**TODAY, AFFIRM THAT YOU ARE GIFTED.
THINK ABOUT WHAT YOUR GIFTS ARE.
IDENTIFY YOUR GIFTS AND CLAIM THEM.**

The belief that we are gifted hardly ever crosses most people's minds. We think the term "gifted" is reserved for entertainers, geniuses, athletes and musicians like Michael Jordan, Jay-Z or Stevie Wonder. We think to be considered gifted, we must first be recognized by the masses for a great achievement. But that's not all true. The truth is that all of us have gifts and talents. Your gifts were given to you at birth. You must come to know and believe this. You're uniquely gifted.

> "Even though I walk through the valley of the shadow of death, I will fear no evil for You are with me."
> – Psalm 23:4

TODAY, LEARN TO BE COMFORTABLE WITH YOU. LEARN TO LOVE YOU AND ENJOY YOU.

LEARN TO LET YOU BE THE BEST FRIEND AND COMPANION YOU HAVE. THEN, LET IT BE KNOWN — "I'M NOT ALONE. I AM WITH ME AND GOD."

Let's do some reflection. Do you avoid being by yourself? Do you need the sound of the TV or the radio when you're home alone? Do you need someone to accompany you whenever you go shopping? Does the thought of going home to an empty house or apartment frustrate you? Do you feel left out because you don't have anybody to call your own? Does it hurt or offend you when someone asks how come you're not married? If you answered "yes" to any of these questions, you might be experiencing loneliness. This feeling of loneliness has its origins in our belief that we are alone. The reality is we are never really alone. You are always with at least two other persons — God and you.

> "Your beauty should not come from outward adornment... it should be that of your inner self, the unfading beauty of a gentle and quiet spirit..."
>
> – 1 Peter 3:3-4

TODAY AND GOING FORWARD, WHENEVER ANYONE CALLS YOU OLD-FASHIONED, SMILE.

THEY'VE JUST CONFIRMED THAT YOU ARE ON THE CUTTING EDGE BECAUSE YOU NEVER GO OUT OF STYLE.

Fashion trends come and go each season. Trends come in and out at the speed of light. The latest gadgets have prominent positions in the store while last year's models get thrown into bins as closeouts. Personal prestige rises and falls with the model year of the owner's car. Young men become social outcasts for not wearing the latest sneakers. With all this emphasis on style and fashion, is it surprising that one of the greatest put-downs is to be accused of being old-fashioned or out of style? To call a person old-fashioned is to insinuate that they are unable to keep up with the times. To avoid the negative stigma of being labeled as old-fashioned, we break our necks and our bank accounts trying to keep up with everyone else. The pursuit of acceptance and approval might even become the driving force of our lives. To avoid this pitfall, we must get another perspective on "old-fashioned." The truth is that old-fashioned is the only thing that never goes out of style. That's right. Old fashion is more than a passing craze. It has longevity and can stand the test of time. To be old-fashioned means you never go out of style because you set your own trend. Old-fashioned is always going to be around.

> "Let each of you look not only to his own interests, but also to the interests of others."
> – Philippians 2:4

TODAY, THERE WILL BE OPPORTUNITIES TO "*PRESERVE*" SOMEONE.

**WHEN IT HAPPENS, STEP UP.
WHATEVER YOU CAN DO TO HELP, DO IT.
WHAT YOU DO FOR THEM,
YOU DO FOR YOURSELF.**

Many times, we hear people say, "Self-preservation is the first order of things." Sounds good, but does it really work? Look around and you'll see much evidence of the negative results of people putting self-interest and selfishness above the interest of the group. How about a new paradigm? What if we started to believe and think that the preservation of others is the first order of things? You see, by looking out for others, we ultimately look out for ourselves. By preserving others, we preserve ourselves.

> "And let us not weary of doing good, for in due season
> we will reap
> if we do not give up."
> - Galatians 6:9

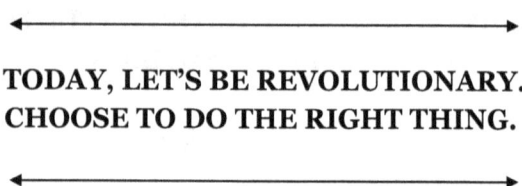

**TODAY, LET'S BE REVOLUTIONARY.
CHOOSE TO DO THE RIGHT THING.**

To many people, being revolutionary means to raise hell and revolt against mainstream traditions and practices. Many believe that breaking laws and defying authority is revolutionary. People revel in their ability to go contrary to things just for the sake of being contrary. They get a false sense of power. The ego gets inflated and they believe themselves to be big and important. This kind of revolutionary is not progressive or productive. To be a true revolutionary in this day and age you must do the right thing — the real right thing.

> "My command is this: Love each other as I have loved you."
> – John 15:12

TODAY, LET US THINK ABOUT LOVE — WHAT IT IS, WHAT IT MEANS, AND HOW WE CAN GIVE IT.

If you ask ten people to define love, you might get ten different responses. Which one is correct? Luckily, we don't have to debate and judge their definitions. There is a source that we can check. Let's see what the scriptures say about love and what it looks like.

"Love is patient and kind; love does not envy or boast; it is not arrogant or rude. It does not insist on its own way. It is not irritable or resentful; it does not rejoice at wrongdoing but rejoices with the truth. Love bears all things, believes all things, hopes all things, endures all things. Love never ends... So now faith, hope and love abide, these three; but the greatest of these is love." (1 Corinthians 13: 4-13 ESV).

You don't have to be religious to connect with this definition. Now you have a reliable definition of love, and clarity on what it should look like. Let's love.

> **"I am the light of the world."**
> – Matthew 5:14

TODAY, I DECLARE THAT I AM A SELF-RESPECTING, LOVING, KIND, DIGNIFIED, AND STRONG MAN. I DECLARE IT AND I WILL ACT LIKE IT.

Nations declare war against each other. People declare their freedom to do, say, think, feel, and believe as they choose. What do you declare? Today, declare all the good things that are true about you.

> "But now you must put them all away: anger, wrath, malice, slander, and obscene talk from your mouth."
> – Colossians 3:8

TODAY, LET'S DOUBLE OUR EFFORTS IN OVERCOMING ANY NEGATIVE FEELINGS ABOUT CERTAIN INSTITUTIONS.

MAKE PEACE WITH THE NEGATIVE AND ACKNOWLEDGE THE POSITIVE.

When we consider the injustice, inequity, brutality, racial bias, and unfair treatment many of us face every day, emotions run high. The pain in our history sometime makes us see through the lens of anger and resentment. One of the results of our emotional upheaval is that we lose the ability to be objective in our evaluation of certain situations. Let's take police brutality, for example. It is real and prevalent. The institution of law-enforcement can be unequal and some individuals may be dishonorable in the way they do their jobs. But not all police officers are brutal and law enforcement, in itself, is honorable and respectable. Become aware of your biases and any lens you use that limits your objectivity. Make a decision to be more balanced in your judgements. Even though we recognize and acknowledge the bad, also give honor to truth by recognizing that there is much good.

> "For we can do nothing against
> the truth, but only for the truth."
>
> – 2 Corinthians 13:8

TODAY, I WILL FACE WHATEVER MY CIRCUMSTANCES ARE AND I WON'T ALLOW OTHERS TO LABEL ME AS PARANOID.

A lot of people expect us to suck it up, grin and bear it. They diminish our experience and tell us, it's not as bad as we think or say it is. But those people have not shared our experience. You can and should identify that the challenges you face – racism, ageism, injustice, housing discrimination, unequal employment or others not listed here, are real. They're not just a figment of your imagination. It can be hell for some people sometimes. Facing and acknowledging our reality does not make us paranoid. But denying reality might make us crazy. Stay sane.

> "A man without self-control is
> like a city broken into
> and left without walls."
>
> – Proverbs 25:28

TODAY, THINK ABOUT HOW TO AVOID GETTING CAUGHT IN ANY EMOTIONAL TRAPS THAT COME OUR WAY. IF THEY COME, REMEMBER HOW TO AVOID GETTING CAUGHT UP AND WALK AWAY.

It seems we don't have to go looking for trouble. Sometimes it comes looking for us. When trouble comes, fortunately, it usually comes with a warning. It usually reveals itself. You can see it coming. This is the bait that tries to get us to bite. It knows if we take the bait, it can hook us. And if it hooks us, we could be in deep trouble. We might react in a way we might regret for a lifetime. So, what do we do when the trouble signals come? We have to be prepared. One strategy is to have a plan in place for those times. A part of that strategy is to know, ahead of time, how we would like to respond to trouble when it pops up. We can think about possible consequences. We can think about how our reaction could impact our lives and the lives of the people we love and care about. In real time, we can consider if it's worth it to feed into the situation, and step off, if we can.

> "From the same mouth comes blessing and cursing. My brothers, these things ought not be so."
> - James 3:10

TODAY I WILL REMOVE MYSELF FROM ENVIRONMENTS WHERE THERE IS TALK THAT DIMINISHES WOMEN.

Whether we call it locker-room talk, man-talk or brush it off by saying "boys will be boys", we all know what it is. Crude talk about women is the type of conversation that lowers men. It lowers men because we are engaging in discussions that use language and images that disparage our sisters and women in general. It's the type of talk that objectifies and devalues women. It doesn't matter if we do it or are just passive listeners when other men do it. Anything that lowers women also lowers us. We lower ourselves when they are lowered. Let's try our best to not use language that does not give honor to women. That's one way I can honor myself.

> "As for you, you meant it for evil against me, but God meant it for good..."
> – Genesis 50:20

TODAY, I WILL EXAMINE MY HURTS AND REMEMBER THAT HURT PEOPLE, HURT PEOPLE. I DON'T WANT TO HURT PEOPLE.

In human relationships, it's virtually impossible to eliminate pain, discomfort and hurt. In fact, much of your personal growth will occur as a result of some kind of painful or uncomfortable experience. Sometimes, the pain we feel are much more severe and damaging than mere growing pains. They may become wounds. At times, they are inflicted on us. Other times, we do the wounding. Whenever someone hurts or wounds another, a likely reason is that the person himself is hurting about something. How do we reduce our capacity to hurt or be hurt by others? The first thing is to be aware that beneath any hurtful act or reaction to another, is our own underlying hurt. Next, we must identify what our own hurts are and start working on them.

> **"It is the hard-working farmer who ought to have the first share of the crop."**
> – 2 Timothy 2:6

TODAY, THINK ABOUT HOW YOU VIEW HARD WORK. ARE YOU MISSING SOME OPPORTUNITY TO GROW, LEARN AND EARN?

Many of us face the prospect of hard work or a challenging assignment with a certain amount of reluctance. We've been trained to seek the easier, more convenient way. We wonder if our given task is more difficult than what's been given to someone else. We may even ask ourselves if we are being overworked. Is this task within my job description? Am I being adequately compensated? We're suspicious of hard work and of the people who give it to us. Changing our attitude toward hard work can open up windows of blessings. Hard work provides opportunities for us to showcase our skills and talents. Hard workers are valuable assets who are more likely than other people to pick the fruits of their labor.

> "O man, what is good: and what does God require of you but to do justice, love kindness, and to walk humbly with your God."
> – Micah 6:8

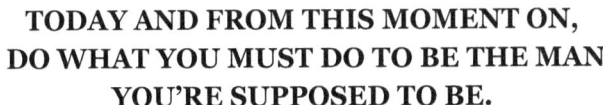

TODAY AND FROM THIS MOMENT ON, DO WHAT YOU MUST DO TO BE THE MAN YOU'RE SUPPOSED TO BE.

When we were little guys, people didn't usually ask us what *kind* of person we wanted to be when we grew up. It was more about what job we want to *do*. Of course, we told him what we wanted to do. We wanted to arrest bad guys, put out fires, drive trains, fly planes, try cases in court, treat the sick, put a ball through a hoop, or race a car around a track. So very little thought was given to what kind of man we wanted to become. Fortunately, it's never too late to formulate that vision. No one can build a house without first envisioning a plan or a design. Likewise, we can't become real men without developing a vision of what it really means. So, let's relax and bring the vision into view. See a man who is kind and compassionate. One that's respectful and courteous to friends and strangers alike. One who children like to be around. One who mothers hope their sons will emulate. See a man who is unintimidating, comforting to others, and an asset to his community. Let your mind and your thoughts form a picture of a man who is slow to anger, who chooses his words carefully, and is willing to admit when he's wrong. See a man who is not afraid to admit he is scared, hurting or needs help. If the man you see is the man you want to be, then make a commitment to become that kind of man. It's as simple as saying "I am committed to being the best man I can be."

> **"Don't copy the behavior and customs of this world, but let God transform you into being a new person by changing the way you think."**
> – Romans 12:2

TODAY, LET'S THINK ABOUT WHO WE ARE, AND WHERE WE FIT.

THEN PUT OUR ENERGY INTO BEING THE BEST AT WHO WE WERE INTENDED TO BE.

Children and young people are not the only ones affected by peer pressure. Sometimes it seems we adults are just as vulnerable to the pressure to conform to the rest of the herd. Many of us start on a particular course, only to be diverted due to our inability to resist the pull of popular culture. Instead of being and becoming who we really should, we succumb to being who others say we should be. We can't beat them therefore we join them. We wanted to generate change, but we have been changed, and maybe not for the better. We had hoped to be the role model for the young people, but we became their imitators. We were supposed to set the standard, and now we're trying to keep up with other people's standard. We attach ourselves to every fad and latch onto every trend. We call it "keeping up with the times." It appears that the world around us has changed our direction and our course. What should we do? We must know who we are and what we're about; what we want and where we want to go; how we are going to get there and who will accompany us on our journey. We must resist latching on to every trend that comes along. Just because something is popular, doesn't mean it's for you.

> **"Let all bitterness and wrath, anger, clamor, and slander be put away from you, along with all malice."**
> - Ephesians 4:31

TODAY, I WILL TRY NOT TO WASTE MY ENERGY DISLIKING OR RESENTING ANYONE.

Picture this: a friend comes to you and tells you that someone you know does not like you. As far as you know, you and that person have always been friendly and cordial to each other. He or she has always treated you well. In fact, you really like this person. Now you've been told they don't like you. How do you respond? Our human response is likely to be that we are not going to like that person either. Never mind the fact that before you heard they don't like you, you had no reason to dislike them. So, why change based on what somebody else says? It takes emotional energy to dislike someone. Why should we use our precious energy to dislike the person just because of what someone tells us? It might be better for us if we try to find out why the person does not like us, assuming you were given correct information. Who knows, maybe they have a reason they think is valid. Certainly, being disliked is not very comfortable. However, disliking someone might be just as uncomfortable. Try to like people.

> "Be like-minded, be sympathetic,
> love one another, be compassionate and humble."
>
> - 1 Peter 3:8

TODAY, I WILL LOOK FOR SOMEONE IN NEED OF COMPASSION AND KINDNESS.

WHEN I FIND THEM, I WILL GIVE THEM THE COMPASSION THEY NEED.

Webster's dictionary defines compassion as "a sympathetic consciousness of other's distress together with a desire to alleviate it." It's amazing and ironic how this great human quality is so frequently looked down on. When we look at our lives, all of us can see instances where we benefited from another person's sympathetic consciousness of our hurts and pains and their desire to help us out of our distress. Their choice to be compassionate benefited us. Even so, in today's culture, compassion has a bad rep. It's seen as soft, sentimental, even weak. Nothing could be further from the truth. To be compassionate is very manly, strong, and powerful. It says that you have the courage to show love and concern for your brothers and sisters. Compassion is a gift we give to others that will always be reciprocated, one way or another. So, don't hold back. Be compassionate.

> "I will instruct you in the way you should go.
> I will council you with my eye upon you."
> - Psalm 32:8

←——————————————————→

TODAY, LET'S THINK ABOUT WHAT WE ARE DOING OR PLANNING TO DO.

IF YOU DON'T WANT THE UNDESIRABLE RESULTS TO HAPPEN, THEN DON'T DO IT.

YOU NEVER KNOW WHEN IT'S GOING TO HAPPEN UNTIL IT HAPPENS.

←——————————————————→

The US Postal Service routinely warns against sending cash in the mail. The police advise us to not leave the door keys under the mat. Anti-auto theft experts preach that we should never leave a car running with the key in the ignition when we are not in it. Yet, with all the cautions and warnings, people still do these things. Have you ever ignored a warning? One reason might be that you did it many times before and got away with it. A feeling of security pervades so you continue, believing the bad outcome will never happen to you. Then, when the unexpected happens you are shocked and surprised. After all, it has never happened before. Our error was in failing to realize that we cannot control when things happen. What we need to understand is that things don't happen before they happen. Whether something happens on the first try or on the tenth, it only happens when it happens, never before or after. So, heed warnings and plan, in advance, so that the likelihood of a bad outcome is lessened.

> "**For the righteous falls seven times and rises again but the wicked stumble in calamity.**"
> - Proverbs 24:16

TODAY, I WILL REMEMBER THAT WHEN I FALL, IT'S ONLY A PART OF THE GLORIOUS JOURNEY TO SUCCESS. I WILL GET UP.

The thought of not succeeding can be frightening. It can delay or discourage any effort to pursue even a desired goal. The fear that someone might see or hear about our failure can also make us abandon lifelong ambitions. We fear that if we pursue a project, each obstacle, or disappointment along the way may be viewed as a sign of failure. But, if we are to ever achieve or accomplish anything, we must be willing to experience and endure failure on the road to eventual success. The common testimony of those who have succeeded at their attempts is that it would not have happened if they had allowed failure to stop their progress. Many attest that each success was preceded by numerous failures. Each time they fell, they got right back up. None achieved success without prior failures. Where was the glory in their journey? The glory was in the fact that each time they fell, they got right up and kept going. Let us keep getting back up too.

> **"Husbands, love your wives, as Christ loved the Church and gave Himself up for her."**
> - Ephesians 5:25

TODAY, LET'S TEACH OUR SONS HOW TO TREAT THEIR WIVES. TODAY, I WILL LET THEM SEE HOW WELL I TREAT MINE.

There is no arguing the fact that the environment in which we were raised sets the bar for the environment we will create to raise our kids in. What went on between our parents will influence what goes on between our wives and us. As our sons observe and internalize the manner in which we treat their mother, that might be how they treat their wives. Furthermore, the way we treat any significant person in our lives determines the quality of our own lives. What we give off comes back to us. So much is at stake. If we want the best for our sons — and we do — then we must teach them to treat their wives in a loving, caring and respectful manner. How do we do this? Let them see us treat their mothers in a loving, caring and respectful manner.

> "**But the fruit of the spirit is love, joy, peace patience, kindness, goodness, faithfulness, gentleness, self-control; against such things, there is no law.**"
> – Galatians 5:22-23

TODAY, I'LL THINK ABOUT WHAT SPIRITUALITY AND LIVING A SPIRITUAL LIFE MEAN TO ME.

Spirituality, or anything hinting of a connection to God, gets a bad rap in our material, man-centered society. Those perceived as spiritual are smeared as weak, needy or dependent. There are many men who think it is okay for women to go to church every Sunday, but a man's masculinity and strength comes into question if he does the same. Those who would even infer that having a relationship with God is a life of weakness for weak people, are completely wrong. Spirituality makes us strong. Spiritual or god-centered people have a sense of what life is about, a sense of direction, and a life of order that's unfamiliar to unspiritual people. Spirituality is the essence of truth and power. If you are already living the spiritual life, keep living it. If you're thinking about pursuing a spiritual way of life, go for it now. Don't allow people to separate you or keep you away from your Source-God. Spirituality is the way of strength, period.

> "For I know the plans I have for you, says the Lord,
> plans for peace and not for evil,
> to give you a future and a hope."
> – Jeremiah 29:11

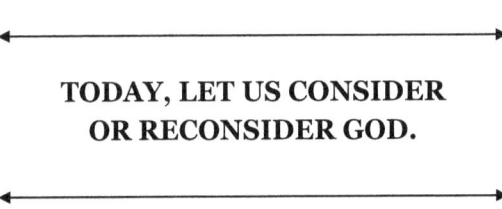

TODAY, LET US CONSIDER OR RECONSIDER GOD.

There is something about our culture today that is so hostile toward having a relationship with God. To believe in God and proclaim that belief is frequently met with cynicism and contempt. Those who live by faith and acknowledge their dependence on a "Higher Power" are viewed with skepticism and considered odd or strange. But when we examine the lives of people who have an active relationship with God and participate in true religious practice, we must admit their lives seem to be marked by a degree of order and stability that many others don't have. This doesn't mean their lives are perfect. If you have a relationship with your God, continue to develop and grow it. If you are someone who doesn't have a connection to a religion, church or spirituality, maybe it's time to give thought to how a relationship with God may enhance your life.

> **"Look carefully then how you walk, not as unwise but as wise."**
> – Ephesians 5:15

TODAY I WILL THINK ABOUT WHAT I'M ABOUT.

If you were asked, what is your life principle, what would your answer be? Your life principle is the way you see things. It's your point of view. It's your beliefs, morals, convictions, and values. It's the standard by which you live. Your life principle determines how you conduct yourself. It's who you are. So, what is your life principle? Is it to live by the golden rule — treat others as you would have them treat you? Is it to get all you can, any way you can? Are you about taking the easier, more convenient route or do you believe in rolling up your sleeves to get the job done? Are you about putting people first, or are personal achievements and material acquisition the driving force of your life? What is your life principle? What are you about? Finding the answer is worth the effort.

> "So let us pursue what makes for peace
> and for mutual up-building."
>
> – Romans 14:19

**TODAY, I WILL REMEMBER
THAT EVERYBODY HAS THE RIGHT
TO BE WRONG AND LET THEM BE.
I DON'T NEED TO WIN AN ARGUMENT.**

Why is it that when we know someone is wrong we feel compelled to let him or her know it? Why must we always win an argument? Why is it that when someone has a different opinion from ours, we go to any length to get him to see things the way we do? Why do other people's mistakes have the power to trip us up emotionally? Why do we need to right everybody's wrong anyway? Why do we persist in denying people their right to be wrong? If they're wrong, so be it. That's their right and it's not your responsibility to point it out.

> **"Create in me a clean heart, O God, and renew a right spirit within me."**
> - Psalm 51:10

TODAY, I WILL LOOK AT ONE THING THAT I WOULD LIKE TO CHANGE AND MAKE A PLAN TO DO WHAT IS NECESSARY FOR CHANGE.

None of us is perfect. We know that is the truth. But is this any justification for not trying to be the best we can be? Many times, we allow ourselves to settle for being who others would approve of. Sometimes we want to be different, to do things that are unpopular, but we give in to the pressure put on us by the crowd. Then we try to justify our weakness or convince ourselves that the behavior is okay. But deep inside we know it's not. We yearn to do better but can't see making a change. There is hope. The mere fact that you can see that things could be better, simply says you could do better if you try. But remember, change always begins with a decision. So, let's decide to change something.

> "**Strength and honor are her clothing; she is confident about the future.**"
> –Proverbs 31:25

TODAY, I WILL GIVE SERIOUS THOUGHT ABOUT MY VIEWS AND ATTITUDES ABOUT FEMALES.

History has led us down a bad road. That road has led to the objectification and lack of appreciation of the value of women. Most men are more likely to see them in ways we would never want another man to see our mothers, sisters, nieces or daughters. This is something we as men should examine and try to change. When we look at women, let us try to look at them the same way we would like men to look at our women, our sisters, mothers, or our daughters. Look at them with respect.

> "An intelligent heart acquires knowledge,
> and the ear of the wise seeks knowledge."
> – Proverbs 18:15

TODAY, I WILL LEARN WHATEVER LESSON I NEED TO LEARN.

THERE IS NEVER A WRONG TIME TO LEARN ANYTHING.

We don't all learn at the same pace. There are many things you still have yet to learn even though you think you should have grasped them years ago. We get so down on ourselves for not doing things we think we should have already done. Sometimes we tell ourselves that it's too late now; that it would not make a difference or be worth it now. We tell ourselves that we are too old, and that we have run out of time. But in our hearts, we know how important the goal is to us. The truth is, if it means so much that you still wish you had done it, now is the time to do it. It's never too late.

> "The prudent sees danger and hides himself,
> but the simple go on and suffer for it."
> - Proverbs 22:3

TODAY, BEFORE WE DO ANYTHING DESTRUCTIVE, LET'S THINK IT THROUGH.

Sometimes we're going to be plain mad at each other. Folks are going to stop talking to each other. There are times we might lose our peace and our patience will be stretched to the limit because of what somebody said or did. There will always be some hurt feelings and some strained relationships. There are a million different ways your buttons can be pushed daily. When it happens, you may naturally wish to retaliate. You want to tear something down or hurt someone. The prospect of revenge seems quite tempting. But can you afford to lose control? Can you really harm another person, without hurting yourself in the process? The answer is, simply, no. There is no excuse for responding in a destructive way.

> "Why, even the hairs on your head are numbered. Fear not; you are of more value than many sparrows."
> – Luke 12:7

TODAY, DON'T COMPARE YOURSELF TO ANYONE. STRIVE TO BE THE BEST YOU CAN BE AND MAKE THE BEST OF EVERYTHING YOU ARE BLESSED WITH.

Comparing ourselves to others is a self-defeating practice. Yet, it's something we do on so many levels. We compare our looks, our wardrobe, height, intellect and position to those around us. The result of comparison is that we either come out better or less than the other person. The reality is that there is really no comparison. Each of us looks the way we look, have what we have and so on. No one can dress like you do or look like you do. You are incomparable. You were made unique and special, just like everyone else. Your complexion, hair, the shape of your nose, and other physical features are custom-made for you. Other people's attributes are unique to them. Nobody can be a better you than you. Nobody can look better than you. You are the best version of you. Believe that.

> "Behold, you are beautiful, my beloved;
> behold you are beautiful; your eyes are doves."
> - Solomon 1:15

TODAY, AS EARLY IN THE DAY AS POSSIBLE, TELL HER YOU LOVE HER.

DON'T WORRY ABOUT HOW IT FEELS OR SOUNDS. JUST SAY IT. "I LOVE YOU."

If saying, "I love you" to your wife, woman, kids or friends is a challenge, welcome to the club. The words seem to be somewhat hard for us men to say to someone, even privately. We no doubt love, but telling it is another matter. Why is this so? Do we find it embarrassing? Do we see that as soft? Do we think it will make us look weak? Is it due to our upbringing and how we were socialized? This needs to change because the people who love us need to hear us tell them we love them. They need to hear it verbally. They may in fact know we truly love them based on how we treat them, but they still need and want to hear us tell them what we feel. So while we try to figure out why we have a hard time saying it, let's start saying it.

> "Ask, and it will be given to you;
> seek and you will find; knock,
> and it will be opened to you."
> –Matthew 7:7

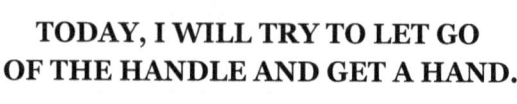

**TODAY, I WILL TRY TO LET GO
OF THE HANDLE AND GET A HAND.**

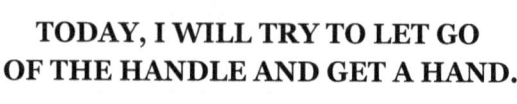

As men, denial of our emotional needs is a major part of our psyche. We are discouraged from admitting, even to ourselves, when our emotional reserves are near depletion. We have bought into the idea that we should be able to handle our business. But handling it is not the issue. The issue is, we are human, not superhuman. We are men, not machines. If we are men and not machines, human not supermen, then it is impossible that we'll be able to handle everything that comes our way. Still, we try to handle things by ourselves. But our experience proves we can't. How do we avoid boiling in this pressure cooker of the "I can handle it" syndrome? We must know and accept the truth that we weren't made to go to it alone. We must admit it to ourselves and ask for help when we need it.

> **"And he said to them, let's go to a quiet place and rest a while."**
> - Mark 6:31

TODAY, LET'S REMOVE AS MANY SOURCES OF NOISE AS POSSIBLE.

Whether we live in a big bustling city or in the most rural area, we live with noise. We grow up with noise. It comes from the loud music, motor vehicles, construction equipment; you name it. We have become so used to noise, many of us go to sleep with the TV or radio on. The constant presence of noise brings to mind a saying: "it's so loud I can't even hear myself think." Imagine being in so much noise that your thoughts are drowned out. This is not healthy for the spirit or the soul. We need silence sometimes. We need quiet. We must have times where there is calm and peace. We need these quiet moments to think, reflect and truly relax with ourselves. We need silence so we can hear. Turn off the TV or radio. Remove the AirPods. Turn the music down. Let us give ourselves the gift of quietness so we can hear ourselves think.

> **"Brothers and sisters, do not be children [immature, childlike] in your thinking; be infants in [matters of] evil [completely innocent and inexperienced], but in your minds be mature [adults]**
> - 1 Corinthians 14:20

**SO TODAY I WILL CHOOSE RIGHTLY.
I WILL CHOOSE MANHOOD.**

Someone once said the only thing you have to do to know you're a male is to look down. Determined at conception, we had no say or choice in the matter. Manhood, on the other hand, might be more a matter of choice. It's a matter of choice because the qualifications of manhood are achieved by consciously choosing to pursue and develop them in us. We choose to be responsible. We choose to be unselfish and considerate toward our fellows. We choose to demonstrate compassion and loyalty. We choose to be law-abiding and obedient to authority. We choose to respect women and be positive role models to children. Yes, we earn the right to be called men, by the choices we make.

> **"A cheerful heart brings a smile to your face; a sad heart makes it hard to get through the day."**
> – Proverbs 15:13

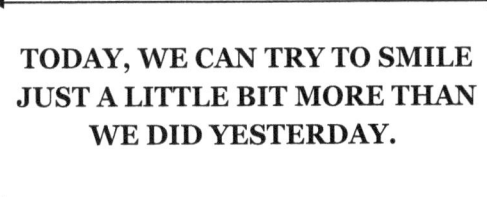

TODAY, WE CAN TRY TO SMILE JUST A LITTLE BIT MORE THAN WE DID YESTERDAY.

Many of the important things in life are free. Take a look at a smile. A smile can increase the good feeling that caused the smile in the first place. A smile can relax a pretty girl's heart. It can make a child feel safe enough to trust you. A smile can tell an employer he'd like having you on the team. It can announce to the world that it's a pleasure having you as a part of it. A smile can even boost the immune system, lower your blood pressure and promote heart health. A smile can do so much, yet doesn't cost a cent. Even more than that, it actually pays to smile.

> **"Love one another with brotherly affection. Outdo one another in showing honor."**
> – Romans 12:10

TODAY I WILL BE NICE TO PEOPLE WHETHER I LIKE OR DISLIKE THEM.

The golden rule says, do unto others, as you would have them do unto you. But so few of us sincerely practice this principle, it very well might be one of the most widely broken laws. Most people tend to treat others the way they feel about them. If they like you, they're nice and friendly. If they don't, then you better watch out. Treating people well only when you like them is a shallow premise, which eventually does more damage to the one who practices it. The reality is that our feelings frequently change, moment-to-moment, day-to-day. So, the same people we like today, we might dislike tomorrow. Therefore we may end up treating them well one day and bad the next. Certainly, this is not a wise approach to life. We need to consciously decide that we are going to try our best to treat people as well as we would like them to treat us. We would not like them to treat us according to how they feel. So, whether we like them or not, let's treat them good.

> "**Whoever brings blessings will be enriched, and one who waters will himself be watered.**"
> - Proverbs 11:25

TODAY, FIND SOMEONE TO HELP SIMPLY BECAUSE THEY NEED IT AND YOU CAN DO IT.

Though help exists in abundance, it is not always readily extended. We might withhold help because the one in need is neither friend nor family nor even known to us. We might withhold it because we think our help doesn't matter, or they can do without it; or maybe someone else will help. It seems we must have a compelling reason before we extend our help. We shouldn't need to have a special reason to help someone? Would we like it if others couldn't find good enough reasons to help us? Of course not. Then let's help someone just because we can.

> "For we aim at what is honorable not only in the Lord's sight but also in the sight of man."
> – 2 Corinthians 8:21

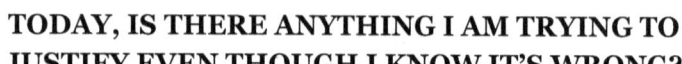

TODAY, IS THERE ANYTHING I AM TRYING TO JUSTIFY EVEN THOUGH I KNOW IT'S WRONG?

INSTEAD OF TRYING TO FIND A RIGHT WAY TO DO A WRONG THING, LET'S TRY TO FIND WAYS TO RIGHT OUR WRONGS.

As human beings, we have a great tendency to rationalize and justify our actions. Each person thinks he's right, and the other person is wrong. And of course the other person thinks he's the right one. Given this natural tendency to believe ourselves right, it becomes difficult for us to resist that inner urge to do something, even when we know, in our minds that it is the wrong action to take. Sure, we know intellectually, it's wrong, but often, our minds go into overdrive to figure out how we can come up with the right reason or justification to do this wrong thing. The store cashier gives us more change than we are due; we decide to keep it because "he's probably overpriced anyway." We taste cherry after cherry in the produce section and see nothing wrong with it, since we're going to buy some. No matter what the excuse, bottom line is, it's wrong. How can we make it right? We can't, because, there is no right way to do a wrong thing.

> "A man who is kind benefits himself,
> but a cruel man hurts himself."
> - Proverbs 11:17

**TODAY, LET'S BE KIND AND
SEE HOW ATTRACTIVE IT MAKES US.**

We men, regardless of background, have a lot in common. We have forever been trying to find that ultimate way to the ladies' hearts and minds. We work on our game, believing the gift of gab will get us over. We work on our physiques because we heard that's what will do the trick. We buy expensive luxury cars to attract the ladies. We flash cash because that's supposed to pull them in. Each of these strategies only works sometime, with some people. But there is something that is guaranteed to make a man attractive to women. That thing is kindness. Yes, kindness makes a man attractive. So, be kind.

> "Beloved, I pray that all may go well with you
> and that you may be in good health,
> as it goes well with your soul."
> - 3 John 1:2

TODAY, LET'S TRY TO EAT SOMETHING TASTY BUT NUTRITIOUS. TRY TO TREAT THAT BODY RIGHT.

Most of us have to admit that our diets are determined by how good the food taste. A lot of what we eat is not wholesome or nutritious. But it's really not about dietary choices. It's really about how much we value our bodies and ultimately our lives. There's nothing wrong with good tasting food, but we got to think about how good for us the food is. Our body is our temple. We have to take care of it. We have to put a high value on our lives. Treat that body right

> "**Do not make friends with a hot-tempered person,
> do not associate with one easily anggered,
> or you may learn their ways
> and get yourself snared.**"
> – Proverbs 22:24-25

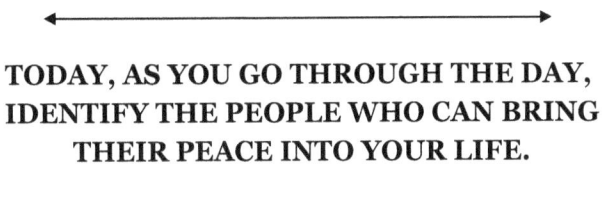

TODAY, AS YOU GO THROUGH THE DAY, IDENTIFY THE PEOPLE WHO CAN BRING THEIR PEACE INTO YOUR LIFE.

Webster's dictionary defines a peacemaker as one who makes peace, especially by reconciling parties in conflict. Does that sound like you? If it does, you are ahead of a lot of people in society. Far too many people are about discord and discontent. Many people's temperaments and attitudes lean more toward aggression and disharmony instead of peace and unity with their brothers. For people who want peace, it's absolutely necessary to seek out people who want the same. Make peace with the world and everyone you cross paths with. Remember, peacemakers will prosper.

> "No foul language should come from your mouth, but only what is good for the building up someone in need, so that it gives grace to those who hear."
> – Ephesians 4:29

TODAY, I'LL GIVE THOUGHT TO MY LANGUAGE AND THE THINGS I SAY.

I'LL THINK BEFORE I SPEAK, AND WHEN I DO, I'M GOING TO KEEP IT CLEAN.

Every individual is unique, in a sense, but there is still much we have in common. We have a common influence on our behavior and attitudes that come from the culture we are raised in. In our culture, men are encouraged to be macho and tough. One of the outcomes of this is that we come to see the use of profanity as a measure of masculinity. Think about that. What does being able to curse have to do with manhood? Nothing. But we see it everywhere- in the club, locker-room, in the streets. Consider profanity from another angle — could it be a lack of vocabulary or indifference to what it might be saying about us? Or could it be due to a lack of discipline? No matter how you look at it, cussing isn't cool. Let's try to keep it clean.

> "Do you not know that you are God's temple and that God's Spirit dwells in you?"
>
> - 1 Corinthians 6:19

TODAY, LET'S BE WITH PEOPLE WHO CAN HELP US BE; PEOPLE WHO WILL HELP US BECOME THE BEST WE CAN BE. LET US BE OUR BEST.

Do you know who you are? Do you know what you are about? Do you have a vision of where you're going and how to get there? At your very core, what's important to you? In your innermost being, what do you want for yourself? Is it fortune and fame? Is it peace of mind and contentment? Is it prominence or obscurity? What are the desires of your heart? These are but a few of the questions we might ask to uncover the nature and essence of who we are. When we find out who we are, we must seek out and be with those who will help us be who we were meant to be. Be with those who help your being.

> "Be careful, then, how you live
> – not as unwise, but as wise, making
> the most of every opportunity,
> because the days are evil."
>
> – Ephesians 5:15-16

TODAY, LET'S KEEP IN MIND THAT WE CAN PAY NOW OR PAY LATER.

HOWEVER, IF WE PAY NOW WE CAN PLAY LATER.

Everything, or at least most things, comes with a price tag attached. The price we pay for what we get might be emotional or financial. Some things might cost us our peace, our joy, our bank account, or our future security. Many times we pay a much higher price than we had to. A primary reason for this higher cost is the timing of our payment. When we put off taking care of the business at hand, interest accrues. What could have been resolved or paid for with a relatively small financial or emotional investment, now requires a major investment of time and resources. Whether we choose to pay now or later, eventually we must pay. So why not pay our dues now so we can play later.

> "And endurance produces character,
> and character produces hope."
>
> – Romans 5:4

TODAY, BE GRATEFUL FOR FAILURES BECAUSE THEY ARE THE BUILDING BLOCKS OF SUCCESS.

We all want to look good to everyone at all times. We are embarrassed when they see us stumble. If we lose our cool or blow our top we die a little inside. Intellectually, we know that we're human and humans make mistakes. However, being comfortable with our humanness is challenging when it seems the world is ready to laugh at our slightest error. The desires of our heart move us toward our goal, but the fear of not getting it right keeps us standing still. We wish we could get to our destination without feeling the pain of failure that could meet us along the way. Often, successes we achieve are built mainly on the failures we experience. We might look or feel silly, but that's OK. We try again. We might have to step back to go forward. No one grows looking cool all the time. So, if your knees get a little wobbly, if you look a little silly, or if you are shamefully embarrassed due to a mistake you made, it's ok. You're growing. Remember, growth isn't graceful.

> "For I am sure that neither death nor life, nor angels, nor rulers, nor things present nor things to come, nor powers, nor height nor depth, nor anything else in all creation, will be able to separate us from the love of God in Christ Jesus our Lord."
> – Romans 8:38-39

TODAY, I WILL REMEMBER THAT I HAVE WORTH AND VALUE. TODAY, I WILL KEEP MY MIND AND MY SIGHT ON MY SELF-WORTH AND BE GRATEFUL FOR IT.

One dictionary defines self-esteem as confidence and satisfaction in oneself or self-respect. In a real sense, self-esteem usually goes along with how good we look or how much money we have. Self-esteem is attached to something external. The thing about self-esteem is it's not always stable. It can change depending on the circumstances or situations that are happening in our lives. If we lose a job or get a new ride, our self-esteem goes down and up, respectively. On the other hand, our worth is something that cannot be changed. We are all born with it. Our worth is a value that cannot be changed by anything or anyone. It is God-given. You can never lose your self-worth. You can only lose sight of it. Always keep your worth in view.

> "This is the day that the Lord has made;
> let us rejoice and be glad in it."
>
> –Psalm 118:24

**TODAY LET'S LOOK FOR
A GOOD DAY.
IT'S THERE.**

**WE WILL FIND IT IF
WE LOOK FOR IT.**

The day may have yet to unfold, but already we are preoccupied with the trials and problems we see ahead. We dread going out the door because of all the stuff we're going to have to face and deal with. We might be convinced it's going to be a bad day. Sure, we know the reality of the circumstances that await us and how challenging and unsettling they might be. However, bad things don't have to make our day bad. To make any day a good day, we just have to look for the good in it. If we're having trouble finding it, look again, and again. Keep looking for a good day.

> **"Show yourself in all respects to be a model of good works, and in your teaching show integrity, dignity."**
> – Titus 2:7

TODAY, LET'S BRING JOY AND HAPPINESS TO OUR CHILDREN BY TREATING THEIR MOTHERS WITH LOVE.

Few situations generate more sadness and hurt than a child seeing his mother hurt. If mom is all right, chances are the child will be too. If mom is not, chances are the child won't be either. The truth is a child's emotional, mental, and physical wellbeing, is closely linked to that of its mother. So, we need to do whatever is in our power to support her wellbeing. When we give love, care, and support to their mom, we are sending a message to our children that we love them enough to love the person that brought them into this world. This is a message they will never forget. Whenever you think about how much you love your child, also think about how you should love his or her mother. One of the best things to do for your child is to love their mother.

> "Know this, my beloved brothers:
> let every person be quick to hear,
> slow to speak, slow to anger."
>
> – James 1:19

TODAY, LET'S MONITOR OUR THINKING. LET'S ASK OURSELVES, "WHAT AM I THINKING?" LET'S ASK OUR BROTHERS, "HOW'S YOUR THINKING?"

The two questions we can expect to be asked are how are you feeling and how are you doing. Our response might be any variation of "I'm feeling good" or "not good"; "fine" or "not fine"; "doing good" or "not too good." Quite likely, our response is a direct result of what we've been thinking. If I'm thinking about the hurtful things my spouse said last night, of course I'm going to feel hurt. When I think about the disrespectful way my boss and coworker spoke to me, it makes me angry. My thoughts about why some people have more prosperity than I do may generate feelings of jealousy and envy. When I think about all the things I failed at, or didn't do, I may become filled with remorse and regret. Our feelings are directly parallel to our thinking. Therefore, to get wrapped up in the feeling is putting the carriage before the horse. Instead, I need to examine the thoughts I'm thinking. My feelings, my attitude and my mood, depend on my thinking. So when we want to know how we're doing or feeling, we have to check our thinking.

> "Listen to advice and accept instruction,
> that you may gain wisdom in the future."
> - Proverbs 19:20

TODAY, I WILL LISTEN.

One of the more unpleasant situations we may experience comes from irate, angry individuals. Spurred on by their own inner turmoil, people can unleash a verbal assault that is intended to humiliate, overpower or insult. People who do this are people who must have their way and their say in order for them to feel good about themselves. In other words, they like to hear themselves talk. When we face such people, everything within us tells us to go toe-to-toe with them and match them word for word, insult for insult. Before you know it, you have two people in a shouting match which makes no sense. Just how do you handle this type of personality? Simply, bite your tongue. Be cool. Don't say a word. You might wonder how can you stand there and say nothing back. Saying nothing does not mean doing nothing. In fact, you're doing a lot. You're listening. By listening, you will hear how foolish the person sounds. With your silence you will increase the chance that as they talk, they will hear how foolish they sound. Hopefully, this will make them calm down.

> "Therefore, however you want people to treat you, so treat them, for this is the Law and the Prophets."
> - Matthew 7:12

TODAY, LET'S BE INTENTIONAL ABOUT BEING THE TYPE OF GUYS OUR SISTERS WANT TO ENCOUNTER.

Many men presume it is our right to cat call or make unwelcome advances toward women. Many times we mistakenly think they secretly want these advances. If we observe closely, the vast majority of the time, women ignore the guys who do this. They find them annoying and just keep going about their business. They just keep walking, without showing or feeling any respect for the offending person. However, men who resist the urge to holla at every woman that walks by, the men who refrain from openly undressing women in the street, these men are a breath of fresh air to women. Let's be men who can say, *"Hi, good morning. Have a good day"* and leave it at that. You'll make her heart glad, even if she doesn't show it.

> "She is more precious than jewels;
> and nothing you desire can compare with her."
> – Proverbs 3:15

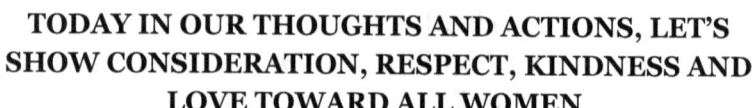

TODAY IN OUR THOUGHTS AND ACTIONS, LET'S SHOW CONSIDERATION, RESPECT, KINDNESS AND LOVE TOWARD ALL WOMEN.

Over the years, there's been growing talk about riffs and schisms between men and women. We hear it all the time. What we don't see or hear much of, is a movement to unite us. We also hear talk about love but little about how we can make love and respect for our sisters a part of our lifestyle. Yes, there is some validity to there being issues between us. That's a societal thing. But we can't let that stop us from proactively showing love and respect to our sisters. As individuals, it's up to us to make a conscious and deliberate decision to build bridges to our women.

> "For each will have to
> bear his own load."
>
> – Galatians 6:5

TODAY, LET'S TRY TO LEAVE PEOPLE AND THEIR PROBLEMS ALONE.

It's human nature to look at the speck in our brother's eye but not at the plank in our own eyes. The other man's faults are much bigger than our own, so we think. How does focusing on another person fault benefit us? It doesn't. It only prevents us from looking at our own issues. Know this: other people's faults are their problems. We've got enough of our own. So, let's keep the focus on ourselves and on the things in us that need working on. Then work on them.

> "Behold, how good and pleasant it is when brothers dwell in unity."
> –Psalm 133:1

TODAY, LET'S THINK ABOUT HOW WE CAN BE A FRIEND. THINK ABOUT WHAT WE CAN DO TO DEMONSTRATE OUR FRIENDSHIP.

Acquaintances come a dime a dozen. Buddies are here today, gone tomorrow. But real friends are a lasting treasure. Like any valuable treasure, true friends are hard to find. In fact, it seems, the more we look for friends the more elusive they seem. But, we need at least one good, real, and true friend in our life. Someone we can talk freely, openly and honestly with. One who will listen carefully without judgment. We need that person we can go to, happy or hurt, knowing for sure they have our best interest in mind. Just how do we get to meet and know such a person? We must first become that person. In other words, we must first learn to be a true friend to ourselves. As we learn how to be our own best friend, we also learn how to be a friend to others. By being a friend to others, you will attract people who desire to be a friend to you. So, if you want to have friends, first be a friend.

> "When I was a child, I spoke like a child,
> I thought like a child, I reasoned like a child.
> When I became a man, I gave up childish things."
> –1 Corinthians 13:11

TODAY, LET'S KEEP IN MIND BOYS DO WHAT THEY WANT.

MEN DO WHAT THEY OUGHT TO DO.

"I do what I want to do. I'm grown."
"Don't tell me what to do. It's my life."
"It's none of your business. I do what I please."

You hear it all the time. These words and ideas have become branded into our cultural psyche. We affirm our adulthood and manhood by our aggressive defense of our right to do our own thing. If doing our own thing coincides with the wishes and desires of others, that's ok. If what we want is in opposition to someone else's interest, too bad for them. We proclaim that we have the right to do what we want. Most of us, if not all, are guilty of displaying this attitude at some time or another. But one good listen to ourselves, followed by an honest admission of what we hear, should convince us of the sheer childishness of our attitude. How childlike it is to always want things our way and hold fast to the belief that we can always do what we want to do. It would benefit us tremendously if we can move toward a more mature position. Don't allow the little boy within you to get free reign anymore. Be the man you can be, by doing what you should do, not just what you want to do.

> "Brothers, join in imitating me,
> and keep your eyes on those who
> walk according to the example
> you have in us."
> – Philippians 3:17

TODAY, I WILL PRACTICE SELF-LEADERSHIP.

I WILL LEAD AND FOLLOW ME IN THE RIGHT DIRECTION.

Talk to most people about leaders and leadership, their concept would be of people who have a following and are able to get people to march the streets with them. If this were always true, then only a small number of us could be leaders. Here is a true story. An eight-year-old boy was asked, *"What is a leader?"* He answered, *"A leader is someone who does the right thing."* By this definition all of us can and should be leaders. If a person can generate enough strength, courage, and character to lead himself in the right direction and to do the right thing, that man is worthy of being called a true leader. Self-leadership is the highest form of leadership. With the ability to lead yourself to do the right thing, there's almost no chance someone could ever lead you to do the wrong thing.

> "Keep a close watch on yourself and on the teaching. Persist in this, for by so doing you will save both yourself and your hearers."
>
> - 1 Timothy 4:16

TODAY, LET US BEGIN TO LOOK AT OUR HIDDEN SELVES SO THAT WE CAN BE IN PRIVATE WHAT WE PROJECT IN PUBLIC.

What do I know about me that I don't want the world to know? All of us have two faces — the one we show to the world and those around us, and the one seen only by ourselves and God. We naturally put our best foot forward for people to see. We modify our speech, attitude and behavior so that we will receive a positive report from our observers. All that's ok. It's only human to desire to be seen in a positive light. However, it is to our advantage to identify those things about us that if they were known, would not make us seem so good after all. And when we find them, we must then admit and accept them. These are the things we will be working on changing about ourselves.

> "But seek first the kingdom of God and His righteousness, and all these things will be added to you."
> - Matthew 6:33

TODAY, LET'S THINK ABOUT THOSE PLEASURES WE CAN POSTPONE UNTIL WE'VE TAKEN CARE OF BUSINESS.

All of us, to some extent or the other, live our lives according to the pleasure principle which is to have as much fun as we can for as long as we can. Since life can be tough and often discouraging, it's understandable how much emphasis we place on having a good time. There is nothing intrinsically wrong with enjoyment. Life shouldn't be a vale of tears, or always somber and serious. However, life is also not always fun and games. We will face unpleasant situations. At times, these unwelcome events compete with things which carry a greater potential for pleasure and immediate gratification. The natural temptation would be to put off the unpleasant stuff in favor of the more gratifying things. This may be a bad move, because what we put off will still be waiting for us, sometimes worse than it was initially. Understandably, choosing to forfeit our pleasures can be difficult. Maybe you shouldn't think of it as depriving yourself of the opportunity for enjoyment. A better way to look at it is that you are just postponing your pleasures while you tend to matters of greater urgency. Postponement means you can later pick up where you left off. Postponing your pleasures in favor of taking care of business will make more pleasure possible in future. Today, learn to postpone your pleasures.

> **"For I will restore health to you,
> and your wounds I will heal,
> declares the Lord."**
>
> – Jeremiah 30:17

TODAY, I'LL SEEK OUT THE HELP I NEED. I'LL SEEK HEALING.

One of the hardest things for a man to admit is that he needs help. It seems against our very nature to acknowledge there might be something wrong with us. We might struggle with anger management, depression, substance-abuse, relationships or low self-image. We might have a few close friends, but in general we find it a challenge getting along with others. People might wonder why you're always in a bad mood or cannot predict the mood you'll be in. Our general attitude may be that life isn't fair, at least not to us. These attitudes are so commonplace that it's often difficult to see that there is something wrong with them. We could be hurting inside and don't know it. And if we do know it, we won't admit it. Could it be that we don't want to be singled out as different? Are we embarrassed to think we are sick while everyone else is all right? We shouldn't be. The fact is all of us; not just some of us, have issues. Therefore all of us — not just some of us — need healing.

> **"So God created man in His own image, in the image of God He created him; male and female He created them."**
> –Genesis 1:27

TODAY, LET'S REMEMBER THAT YOU ARE ROYALTY.

SAY IT WITH YOUR THOUGHTS, SPEECH AND ACTIONS. TODAY, BE THE KING YOU ARE.

One of the greatest lies we've been told and believed is that we are less than. Many of us even believe we are nothing and nobody. That's a lie, period. The fact is, we're born kings. Creator God made us in His image - Kings. Our sisters and mothers are queens. Royal blood courses through our veins, for real. Ever noticed how a king walks? He walks with dignity, confidence and grace. He walks with his head up, not down. There is a natural air about him that says, "I know who I am." Do you know that you are a king? You are, so recognize.

> "Do not neglect to do good and to share what you have; for such sacrifices are pleasing to God."
> – Hebrews 13:16

TODAY, WHAT DO I HAVE OR KNOW THAT I CAN GIVE AWAY?

All of us have something to give that can help the next person. It may be some acquired knowledge or information. It could be wisdom, built up through experiences. The beautiful thing about it is, it doesn't matter your age. Young and old have something to give. If we look closely enough into our lives, we can see we have a lot of special gems and pearls we can share with our fellow man that will make their lives that much better. Pass it on.

> "Gracious words are like a honeycomb,
> sweetness to the soul and
> health to the body."
> - Proverbs 16:24

TODAY, LET'S TRY OUR BEST TO BE KIND, GENTLE AND WARM.

TRY BEING A GENTLE MAN TO HER AND SEE HOW FAR A LITTLE GENTLENESS WILL TAKE YOU. SHE'LL LOVE YOU FOR IT.

To be perceived as soft goes against every grain of how we've been socialized as men. We've been convinced that, at least our exterior must be tough, hard, and even impenetrable. But let's be honest, what we project on the outside isn't always what is happening on the inside. On the inside, we're vulnerable, yearning to lower the facade and take off the mask. On the inside, we wish we could let go of all the macho nonsense. On the inside we want to be able to warm up to our women and freely demonstrate the gentle side of us that we know is there, but we're scared. How do we let the image go? How do we push through the fear? One way is to start small. Try saying something nice to her. Give her a hug. Kiss her when she enters the car. Sounds corny? Try it anyway. Try a little gentleness.

> "Husbands (Men), love your wives (women) and do not be harsh with them."
> –Colossians 3:19

TODAY, IF YOU FEEL THAT BEING TOUGH KEEPS GETTING TOUGHER TO DO, TRY A LITTLE TENDERNESS.

IF YOU FIND IT A LITTLE TOUGH BEING TENDER, TRY A LITTLE HARDER.

Most of us would probably have to admit we would rather be seen as tough than tender. We are taught that softness is an undesirable quality. You have to be tough to make it in this world. We have come to believe that any show of vulnerability is a show of weakness. As ineffectual as it is to be a total push over, it is also counter productive to maintain and nurture a hard-edged attitude towards life. Our own human make-up makes it impossible for us to maintain one hundred percent toughness. The unchangeable fact of our makeup is that none of us is too tough to be tender or too tender to be a little tough. Like it or not, we were designed to be a little bit of both. Let's try a little more tenderness.

> "And we know that for those who love God, all things work together for good, for those who are called according to His purpose."
> – Romans 8:28

TODAY, LET'S KEEP OUR THOUGHTS FOCUSED ON WHAT IS IN FRONT OF US.

LET YESTERDAY GO. DON'T HOLD ON TO THE PAST.

Today is a brand new day. Yesterday is history. Tomorrow is a mystery. Yesterday is gone. We can't go back there. Tomorrow is the future that we don't yet have. The only day in which we can live is today. If we live in yesterday with all the mistakes we made, it could lead to regret, sadness or even depression. If our thoughts are always in tomorrow, this could generate the fear that's associated with the unknown. This doesn't mean we can't reflect and look over our past or anticipate things in the future. What it means is that the main focus of our thinking should be in the present moment. God will take care of our future.

> **"For while bodily training is of some value, godliness is of value in every way, as it holds promise for the present life and also for the life to come."**
> – 1 Timothy 4:8

TODAY, LET'S EXAMINE OUR BELIEFS ABOUT MANHOOD.

WHAT ARE THEY? DO THEY WORK?

The emphasis on toughness is ingrained in the society. A man must be hard. He must not feel, cry, or show emotions. We can't say, "I'm hurting." But it's ok to say, "I'm angry as hell." The truth is we have emotions and feelings just like the opposite sex. After all we're human, right? Much of this mis-education about manhood comes from people who have also been mis-educated. We don't have to continue the cycle of misinformation. We can change our views about manhood to one that's healthy and Godly.

> **"Have nothing to do with foolish, ignorant controversies; you know that they breed quarrels."**
> – 2 Timothy 2:23

TODAY, LET US THINK ABOUT HOW WE CAN SIDESTEP THE EMOTIONAL BOOBY TRAP OF A HEATED ARGUMENT.

LET US TRY TO HANDLE ALL OUR DISAGREEMENTS WITHOUT ACTING IN A DISAGREEABLE MANNER.

Do you remember your last argument? What was it about? How did you and the other party behave? Did anyone say anything they regretted? Could you have avoided it? What did it feel like afterwards? Can you honestly say that you walked away better off than before it started? We never do. Going in, an argument seems like a worthy cause, a justified exercise in defense of our rights. But during and after is where we do damage to ourselves. Our blood vessels constrict, reducing blood flow to the brain, causing the heart to work even harder to pump blood. Adrenaline secretion increases muscle tension. Over secretion of gastric juices, eat at our stomach lining. These physiological changes do damage to the body. So how can I avoid hurting myself today? We must realize that how we act, react or respond to things is our choice. We have a choice whether we take the bait or not. We must also realize that settling conflicts and confrontation does not require combat. Let's agree to disagree without being disagreeable.

> "Fear not, for I am with you;
> be not dismayed, for I am your God;
> I will strengthen you, I will help you,
> I will uphold you with
> my righteous right hand."
>
> – Isaiah 41:10

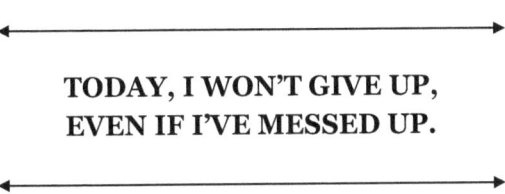

TODAY, I WON'T GIVE UP, EVEN IF I'VE MESSED UP.

Sometimes we can become caught up in a stream of circumstances that puts us in a difficult situation. We might have been living relatively wholesome or even exemplary lives, until one bad move turns our lives inside out. Maybe that fine woman we were dating turns up pregnant. We might have overindulged our pleasures and now we can't meet our financial obligations. It could be that our attitude put us at odds with a certain manager. Or we lost our temper and hit somebody. Whatever mess we got ourselves into, no matter how deep the hole we fell into, or how serious the trouble, there is a solution and a way out. The forces against us will tell us, *"You messed up, so you might as well keep going."* That nasty little voice might whisper, *"What's the use? It's too late to turn back now."* The truth is, no dilemma is insurmountable. Sure, we can't undo what we've done but if we give up, we might not get to clean the mess up. Never give up on you.

> "A person who refuses to admit his mistakes can never be successful. But if that person confesses and forsakes those mistakes, another chance is given."
> – Proverbs 28:13

TODAY, LET'S MAKE LIFE BETTER FOR US. ACCEPT WHEN THE FAULT IS OURS, ADMIT WHEN WE ARE WRONG AND MOVE ON. WE'RE NOT PERFECT.

There was a professional basketball player whose claim to fame was that he never would concede that he committed a foul. Each time he got called, it was the ref's bad call or the other player was the real culprit. Each time they called a foul on him, he protested vehemently, even to the point where he would get a technical added to it. He would always claim the refs were picking on him. Whenever he got tossed from the game, he'd claim it really proved the refs were out to get him. The refs, his coach, teammates, the spectators, the TV audience all saw him foul but he would never admit it. Regardless of his protest, the call still held up. Most likely, we're not as bad as this player. But most of us, like him, have a hard time admitting we're wrong. If only we would accept when we are wrong, we would spare ourselves a lot of trouble and wasted energy. When we're wrong, just admit it and move on.

> "Honor your father and your mother, that your days may be long in the land that your God is giving you."
> –Exodus 20:12

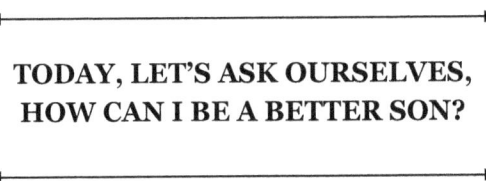

TODAY, LET'S ASK OURSELVES, HOW CAN I BE A BETTER SON?

What kind of son am I? Some of the first people we blame for our condition and circumstances are our parents. We blame them for not giving us enough or for spoiling us too much; for being too strict or too lenient; for not being there or for being too smothering. We tell ourselves that it's dad's fault because he wasn't around. We may think if mother was a different type of woman, we would be better off. Granted, parental influences play a major role in our development, but our behavior, as sons must also be taken into account. Did we listen and cooperate with our parents? Did we break their rules every chance we got? Did we do things to lighten their burdens or did we feel as though they were just there to meet our needs? At some point — like now — we've got to think about what kind of sons we were, are, or want to become. Let's be the best sons we can be.

> "Oh, taste and see that the Lord is good!
> Blessed is the man who takes refuge in him!"
>
> – Psalm 34:8

TODAY, LET'S THINK ABOUT HOW GOOD GOD IS.

When things are going our way, it's not at all difficult to feel gratitude for the good that's happening in our lives. When our dreams are coming true, most of us have no problem thanking God for our blessings. But when things go wrong, and we're not where we want to be, how do we react? As humans, we are likely to feel self-pity. We may complain and bemoan our circumstances. When times were good, we cheered God. Now that times are bad, we jeer Him. How could he do this to me? Sounds familiar? Many of us are like that. The thing to remember is that bad times are going to come. When they arrive, it doesn't mean God became bad. In fact, it is God who will see us through the bad times. He'll be there because He is good even when times are bad. God is good, all the time.

> "Come to me, all who labor and are heavy laden, and I will give you rest."
>
> - Matthew 11:28

TODAY, HERE'S SOMETHING TO CONSIDER. TRY TAKING A PERSONAL DAY OFF BECAUSE YOU FEEL GOOD. IT MAY BE A HEALTHY THING TO DO.

In almost every compensation package, a certain number of days are given to each employee to be used as sick days or personal time off. Sometimes these days are utilized for legitimate illnesses or other health related reasons. However, people who are perfectly fine but want to be off work, often use sick days. When they want a day off the job, they call in sick. Normally, just about everybody tries to avoid getting sick. But when we want time off from work, we claim illness even when we are not. It's somewhat of a paradox- we claim a condition of mind and body we usually want to avoid, when it serves our purpose. Consider for a moment; wouldn't it make better sense to be off while in the best of condition? Why wait till we feel bad? Think about taking the day off when you feel good; and enjoy it.

> "Keep your life free from the love of money; and be content with what you have. For He has said, 'I will never leave you nor forsake you.'"
> – Hebrews 13:5

TODAY, LET'S LOOK AT WHOM WE MIGHT BE JEALOUS OF AND SEE IF THAT PERSON IS SOMEONE WE WOULD REALLY WANT TO BE LIKE.

You've seen them in action: guys who literally spread their money around, kicking the cash to keep ladies happy and comfortable. Their spending is not from kindness or a sense of charity. Rather, they spend money to get the favor and attention of the object of their desires. Though we might see through their motives and methods, we might secretly envy them. Even when we don't operate in the same manner they do, we may wish we had the money they have. Certainly, we might want the things they are able to buy with their funds. Though our envy is real, a quick look at a few facts will help adjust our attitude. First off, there is a name commonly used to identify men who buy a woman's attention. They are called Sugar Daddies. Their money is the honey they use to attract bees. Therefore, if we're jealous of those guys, it's really misdirected because we are in reality envious of a person we really don't want to be like.

> "For what does it profit a man to gain the whole world and forfeit his soul."
>
> – Mark 8:36

TODAY I WILL LOOK AT ALL THAT I AM TO DETERMINE IF I AM TRULY BETTER OFF EVEN WITH ALL THAT I HAVE.

For many of us, the trappings of success are always on display. We live in better neighborhoods. We wear high-end designer clothes. Our incomes may be higher than the average person's. We have the resources to enjoy Caribbean vacations, eat in trendy restaurants and drive luxury imports. Our 401(k) and pension plans are several times higher than what our parents ever had. We are amazed at how far we have come. We have arrived. But with all we have going for ourselves, we still might feel like something's missing. With success, comes more pressure and stress. With more income, comes more debt. With more promotions, ironically, comes more job insecurity. Therefore, we can rightly conclude that having achieved more doesn't mean we are better off.

> **"He heals the brokenhearted and binds up their wounds."**
> – Psalm 147:3

TODAY LET'S LOOK AT THE THINGS AND PEOPLE THAT HURT OUR FEELINGS FROM ANOTHER PERSPECTIVE.

LET'S LOOK AT THEM AS THINGS THAT ARE JUST THERE TO HELP US HEAL.

The saying "no pain no gain" is a guideline many live by in the gym because in our culture, building firm, chiseled bodies is a priority. But outside the gym, pain is a feeling we are taught to avoid or deny. When we experience emotional pain, our likely response is to focus on the person who caused the hurt. Next, we look for ways to hurt them back. We feel justified in lashing out. After all, they hurt us first. Seldom do we see this type of pain or hurt as something arising out of something within us that might need healing. Rarely will we admit there might be something wrong with us. Readily we will affirm there's something the matter with the offender. But pointing the finger of blame does not relieve us of our own pain. Long after the offending one has gone about his or her business, we are still sore and bent out of shape. The solution is to first know the facts: emotional pain is an indication of an area in our lives, which we need to work on. This pain can be viewed in a positive light because it tells us there is something inside of us that needs healing. It might not feel good, but at least we now know it can point to the wounds that we can begin to mend. Anything that hurts our feelings can help with our healing.

> "For everything there is a season,
> and a time for every
> matter under the sun."
>
> – Ecclesiastes 3:1

TODAY, MAKE TIME TO DO WHAT IT IS YOU NEED AND WANT TO DO BUT THOUGHT YOU DIDN'T HAVE THE TIME TO DO IT.

In our busy lives, is it any wonder we can't find time to do certain things we would like to? Each day finds us juggling work, school, family time, travel time, recreation, sleep and a hundred other things. We can sometime feel so overwhelmed with activity, we wish we had more hours in the day. But twenty-four hours is all we get, no more. So, how are we going to find the time we need to do the things we need and like to do? Well, we really don't have to find it. We already have it. We just need to determine where in your schedule to fit this new activity. If you can't find time, then make time.

> **"For God has not given us a spirit of fear and timidity, but of power, love, and self discipline."**
> - 2 Timothy 1:7

TODAY I WILL EXAMINE MY GUTS TO SEE IF I NEED A DIFFERENT KIND.

Our society places a great deal of emphasis on courage and guts. Our heroes seem to all emerge from areas that pit people against each other in tests of strength and stamina. There are ironman contests, battles of the fittest, and survivor. We almost worship the bravest, boldest and finest. Demonstrate a willingness to risk life and limb, and they'll say you have guts. However, as admirable as physical bravery is, there is another kind of guts we need to develop. We might have the guts to fight, but do we have the guts to walk away? We might have guts to speak our minds, but do we have the guts to accept criticism? We may have the guts to point out the truth we see in others, but can we examine ourselves and face what we see? Do we have the guts to stand for what's right at the risk of being unpopular? Do we have the guts to cooperate while everyone else is rebelling?

> "Let me hear in the morning of Your steadfast love,
> for in You I trust. Make me know the way
> I should go, for to You I lift up my soul."
> –Psalm 143:8

TODAY, LET'S LOOK FOR THE PERSON WHO WE TRUST ENOUGH AND BE WILLING TO TELL IT JUST AS IT IS, NOT JUST AS IT SEEMS.

When we run into someone, whether it's a friend or a stranger, there are some standard questions we are sure to be asked. How are you? How are you doing? How are you feeling today? In response to these inquiries, we may give the automatic response, "I am fine!" "I'm doing well." "I'm OK." "I'm all right." However, the way we tell it isn't always the way it is. Sometimes things are not all right. But we're so conditioned to pretend things are good. On the inside, we wish we could come clean and admit we're not doing so well. We're not ok. The one major obstacle is finding someone we trust enough to be real and honest with. We think no one wants to hear our troubles. We think no one would understand. The truth is, there is always someone you can tell whatever is on your mind. There is always someone who understands and is willing to listen. Let's look carefully for that person.

> "As each has received a gift, use it to serve one another, as good stewards of God's varied grace."
> – 1 Peter 4:10

TODAY, WITHOUT COMPARING, IDENTIFY ALL THE ASSETS, TALENTS, AND GIFTS YOU HAVE. COUNT THESE BLESSINGS AND BE GRATEFUL THAT GOD DID NOT LEAVE YOU OUT.

Why am I not smart like Joey? How come I can't play ball as good as the other guys? I should've been more handsome. I wish my parents were rich like John's parents. Why can't I be popular with the girls? Why am I so shy, so fat, so short, or so skinny? Why can't I dance as good as Larry? How come I'm not cool like the guys on my job? It's just not fair. I got a bum deal. Have you ever felt like that? Any comparison of ourselves, our circumstances, or our attributes to someone else is likely to land us in one of two places: either above or below the one we are being compared to. In other words, comparisons make us either greater than or less than. Neither position offers any lasting satisfaction or comfort. So, how do we avoid the heartache associated with the feeling of being less than the next person? We must understand and believe that we all have been given our own special gifts. We all have our own unique set of talents and abilities. We must believe we are special people, created and put here to perform a special role. We bring a lot of value to the world. Regardless of how plain and ordinary we might seem to ourselves, no other person can take our place. Each of us is special because when God gave out his blessings, he didn't forget your share. God didn't leave you out.

> "Casting all your anxieties on Him
> because He cares for you."
> –1 Peter 5:7

TODAY, IF YOU'RE LOOKING FOR OPPORTUNITIES, GATHER UP ALL YOUR PROBLEMS, AND LOOK BEHIND THEM.

What is a problem? Is it an obstacle in our way? Is it something or someone we would rather not deal with? Is it a situation or circumstance we would like to change to something else? Or is it a feeling we would rather not feel — a pain we would rather not sense? Just what is a problem? The better question might be, why is something a problem? Something becomes a problem when we perceive it as a threat to our safety, security, or peace of mind. This perception then causes us to focus only on the negative aspects of the thing or situation causing the issue. Therefore, a problem is really a result of how we look at our circumstance. If we see in our situation, nothing more than an undesirable event to be erased or solved, then we really have a problem. However, when we look to see how we can benefit and gain from this so-called problem, we will see that the problem was just the curtain blocking our view of the opportunities behind them. Behind every problem is an opportunity.

> "And you will know the truth and
> the truth will set you free."
>
> - John 8:32

TODAY, I WILL SEE ANY FEELINGS OR EMOTIONS I FEEL FOR WHAT THEY ARE, JUST FEELINGS.

NO MATTER HOW REAL THEY SEEM, WE WILL NOT LET FEELINGS DEFINE US AND WE WON'T MAKE THEM FACTS.

In this life, we are no strangers to adversity and hostility. There is no denying the truth that we have to contend with a lot of negativity, intentionally or unintentionally directed toward us. This causes feelings of hurt and anger inside us. We may have feelings of inferiority or feelings of inadequacy. It may have happened for so long and so often that we might sometimes wonder if these feelings reflect something true about us. What we must realize is that these are just feelings, not facts about us. We are not inferior or less than. We are very much adequate. Surely, it's a fact that we feel, but feelings are not facts. Remember that.

> "Do not judge by appearances,
> but judge with right judgment."
> – John 7:24

TODAY, I WILL LOOK AT THE STANDARD BY WHICH I'M LIVING.

TODAY, I WILL ASSESS WHETHER IF I'M LIVING UP TO A HIGH STANDARD.

What is my standard of living? In today's material world, economic resources are a measure of one's standard of living. The more money we earn, the higher the standard of living we are perceived to have. According to this perspective, our standard of living rises based on the cost of our houses and cars, the exclusivity of the restaurants we dine in, and the tuition of the schools we send our children to. Much of our energy is directed at maintaining or achieving the highest possible financial and material standard of living we can. But there is another standard by which we may measure our lives. This standard is determined, not by money, but by the level of character, integrity, and emotional and spiritual capital present in our lives. This is the standard that determines how far you would go or what you would do to raise the material standard of living. To check your standard of living, we might ask ourselves questions such as: Am I conscientious about my performance at work? Am I fair in the treatment of my family and friends? What are the things I would not do to get what I want or where I want to go? What are the boundaries I have set for my conduct and behavior? Am I being all that I truly want to be? What do I stand for? What is my standard.

> **"For they loved the glory that comes from man more than the glory that come from God."**
> – John 12:43

TODAY, I WILL ACKNOWLEDGE WHEN I NEED OR WANT ATTENTION.

IF I DO SEEK ATTENTION, I WILL SEEK POSITIVE ATTENTION.

You've seen them before. They always seem to be out front — the life of the party. They are the most vocal ones in the group. They appear to be confident and self-assured. But external appearances don't always reflect internal reality. Contrary to what they project, these are often people who have a strong need for attention. This need for attention can be so controlling, people will sometimes settle for negative attention rather than do without attention. Of course, most of us don't need attention to this extent. However, we all have moments when we want attention. After all, we are human. So, how do we get the attention we need? First, acknowledge the need and admit it. It does not make you weak. Neither does it make you needy. Next, identify the person who you believe you can get the attention you need from. Then reach out to this person.

> "I know that you can do all things,
> and no purpose of yours can be thwarted."
> - Job 42:2

TODAY AND EVERY DAY, I WILL PURPOSELY THINK ABOUT MY PURPOSE.

If you were handing out duties and responsibilities for people you know, what would you assign yourself? Would you make yourself a kindergarten teacher or a music composer? A community activist or a surrogate dad to fatherless kids in the neighborhood? Would you trust yourself to protect the rights of the oppressed? Would your assignment be a captain of industry and finance or to protect and serve in the local Police Department? Do you know your purpose? If you don't, don't feel bad. Many of us don't. Not knowing the specific purpose for us being put here does not diminish you in any way. However, knowing it would give you a greater sense of awareness of who you are, and your value to the world. It will also empower you so you can confidently and boldly walk in that area. The search to find our purpose is a major step toward personal fulfillment. This search begins with the awareness that you do have a purpose. You were not just dropped here, or randomly selected to be alive now. You have a purpose. You have something to offer the world. You have value.

> **"Don't forget where the Lord brought you from."**
> – Deuteronomy 6:12

TODAY THINK ABOUT WHERE YOU HAVE BEEN AND WHERE YOU ARE.

REMEMBER WHERE YOU CAME FROM.

"Don't forget where you came from. You might have to go back there one day." Some of us have heard this warning. You see, many of us come from relatively ordinary beginnings. Very early in life, we are encouraged to strive and persist in order to better ourselves. Along the way, we observe evidence of those who did get ahead but forgot, for a time, where they came from. Some got in trouble. Some became disillusioned and were disappointed to find that the grass wasn't greener on the other side. Their disappointment is telling. It proves that they didn't completely forget their humble beginnings, because they still have a point of reference. The proof is in their ability to compare where they are, where they were and the path in between. So, the problem is not that we forget. The problem is how do we find our way back to our roots, the parts of our history that built and nurtured us into who we are today such as family, old friends, the community we grew up in, or our childhood church. It's so important that we never disconnect from our roots. Don't forget home. But if you do, stop, remember, and find your way back.

> **"A good name is to be more desired than great wealth, (God's) favor is better than silver and gold."**
> – Proverbs 22:1

TODAY, START THINKING ABOUT WHAT YOU WANT YOUR LEGACY TO BE AND WHETHER YOU'RE LIVING THE WAY YOU WANT TO BE KNOWN.

We hear a lot about *legacy* these days. Legacy often comes across like it's something reserved for special people such as world class athletes and celebrity entertainers. *Legacy* is really a universal concept that every single one of us builds as we go and grow through life. Your legacy will include material things like your vehicle and business, but it will also include your character and impact. It's the impact you have had in your community, family, industry, and so on. The thing about our legacy is, we are the ones responsible for it. While we are living, we determine what our legacy will be after we're gone from this earth. Legacy is intentional and speaks to the fruit and impact that remains after consistent efforts in an area. You must live with your legacy in mind. Do you want to be known for being devoted to your family, or for being a father to some but provider of none? Do you want to be remembered as a tough guy who was always quick to fight? Do you want to be known as a positive role model to your children and other youth? Do you want to be remembered as a man with high self-control and self-respect, or as one who was erratic and reckless? What do you want to be known for? Will your children remember you for your thoughtfulness to their mother? Will you be known for being more conscious about the condition of your clothes and car than the wellbeing of your children? When you are no longer here, will your loved ones say it was good to have known you, or good riddance? What will you be known for? Are you a man of your word? Do you want to be known for treating others as you would like them to treat you? How do you hope that persons speak about you behind your back? Be intentional about building your legacy. Building your legacy starts today.

> "Walk in wisdom toward outsiders, making the best use of the time."
> - Colossians 4:5

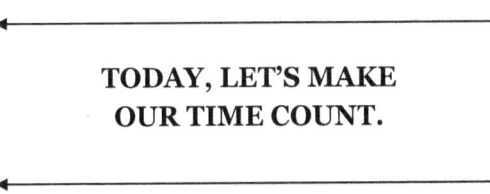

TODAY, LET'S MAKE OUR TIME COUNT.

Time cannot be stored or saved for future use. You cannot bring it back from the past. Time can't be slowed down or sped up. Time cannot be stopped. Once it's gone, it's gone. There are two facts about time that should be understood. One is that, time cannot be controlled or manipulated. The second, is that time is completely fair. No matter how young or old we are, we all have the same amount — right now. So, with the time that we have right now, let's examine how we've been spending our time. Am I spending it in activities that will enhance my life? Am I sharpening my professional skills? Am I nurturing relationships with friends and family? Am I helping my community? Am I making the best use of my time now? Make your time count.

> "I pray that out of his glorious riches he may strengthen you with power through His spirit in your inner being."
> – Ephesians 3:16

TODAY, I WILL THINK OF WAYS I CAN APPLY MY STRENGTH TO BRING GOOD TO MY LIFE AND OTHERS.

We have allowed our fathers, uncles, friends, guys on the block, teammates, and artists to teach us their own misguided definition of a strong man. We have adopted others' opinions of how a strong man should be. They say a strong man never cries. They say a strong man should know how to cuss and fight. They say a strong man should have plenty of women. As men, we have learned to use our strength to intimidate, to manipulate, and to overpower others. We must recognize and accept the fact that we have been misinformed by the misinformed. Now is the time to reject the wrong concepts. Your strength is for helping, not hurting; healing, not harming; repairing, not destroying.

> "All your children will be taught
> by the Lord and great
> will be their peace."
> –Isaiah 54:13

TODAY, LET US GIVE SOME THOUGHT TO SOMETHING WE CAN DO TO MAKE THIS A BETTER WORLD, AND THEN LET US MAKE IT BETTER FOR THE CHILDREN.

Our children didn't ask to come here. They didn't have a choice of parents. In far too many instances, children were unplanned and/or unwanted. Many children are the result of selfish indulgence in our pleasures. Their unpremeditated arrival into this world leads to them being viewed as burdens rather than the treasures they truly are. To top it off, the world we bring them into, as Marvin Gaye said, is enough to "make you wanna holler." But now that they're here, what do we do about it? Without wallowing in unproductive guilt and remorse over a situation we cannot change, we must first acknowledge our responsibility for their care and development. Then, we launch into a plan of action to meet our obligations to them. Sure, we brought them into a harsh world, but we have the opportunity to do our best to make it good for them.

> "But they who wait for the Lord shall renew their strength; they shall mount up with wings like eagles, they shall run and not be weary; they shall walk and not faint."
>
> – Isaiah 40:31

TODAY, LET'S WAIT PATIENTLY. LEARNING TO WAIT HELPS DEVELOP OUR PATIENCE.

Impatience is one of the most devastating characteristics a man can have. It can lead to decisions and actions that have long-term negative impact on our lives, reputations, and relationships. Impatience is often rooted in a strong urge to quickly fulfill a desire or goal. Now, there's nothing wrong with wanting something badly. But wanting it so bad that we throw caution to the wind can be harmful. Impatience can manifest in various ways. It can look like rushing into a marriage. It can look like leaving a job before finding another one. It can look like confronting someone prematurely, just to find out that we had wrong or insufficient information. In all these examples, we should have waited and took our time, but we did not. When things blow up in our faces, we wonder why. So, developing patience is probably one of the most important investments we can make into ourselves. We must work to be patient with others and also be patient with ourselves.

> "We who are strong have an obligation to bear with the failings of the weak, and not to please ourselves."
> – Romans 15:1

TODAY, I WILL REFUSE TO SEE MY BROTHER AS ANYTHING LESS THAN THE CHILD OF GOD THAT HE IS. I WILL SEE HIM EXACTLY AS I WISH TO BE SEEN.

There are men who shun other men who they see as less educated and less well spoken. There are brothers who blush with embarrassment when they encounter a brother who is not as refined or as sophisticated as they think he should be. There are brothers who turn their heads and avert their gaze when a "certain type" of brother approaches. All of us have a little bit of that kind of person in us. Arguably, this might come from our own insecurities. It could also be pointing to our own lack of empathy and sensitivity toward another person's situation. When you look at it, feeling embarrassed about how another person acts, looks or talks, puts us in a position of weakness, not strength. Feeling like he's making us look bad in front of "them," is ascribing way too much power to other people's opinion. Truth is, it might not even matter to whoever "them" is. We're the ones that make it matter. Why should we be embarrassed? Think of something about you that fall short or needs improvement. How would you feel if another man judge you and thought less of you? Would you like being evaluated based on your short comings? Try to feel compassion and understanding toward your brother, regardless of his area of weakness. Stop feeling the need to apologize or be embarrassed about him. Support, affirm and empower him however you can. This strengthens you.

> "What is desired in a man is steadfast love, and a poor man is better than a liar."
>
> – Proverbs 19:22

TODAY, LET'S ACKNOWLEDGE OUR KINDER SIDE BECAUSE IT'S OUR MANLIER SIDE.

THE WOMEN IN OUR LIVES BENEFIT FROM IT AND THEY KNOW STRENGTH WHEN THEY SEE IT.

Try to talk to some men about their "soft" side and you are likely to get push back. Some may think manhood and softness don't go together. They may think washing the dishes, doing laundry or doing the cooking for the family is unmanly. Let's not debate the issue. Let's not get hung up on words. If you have a mother, wife, girlfriend, niece, or female co-worker, you will need to know how to soften your approach. The women in our lives need that side of us. Roughness doesn't work for or with them. I guarantee you that a softer approach would bear better and longer lasting fruit. So, you need to know that what the fellows often see as soft, your women see as strong. They perceive strength in respect, politeness, kindness and chivalry. They see kindness as strong.

> **"But God, being rich in mercy, because of the great love with which He loved us"**
> - Ephesians 2:4

TODAY, EVEN IF NO ONE TELLS YOU THEY LOVE YOU,

TELL YOURSELF YOU ARE LOVABLE.

None of us is perfect. Even if your body was transformed today into the body of your dreams, by tomorrow you would still have insecurities. Even if you were the epitome of style and grace, adhering to all the rules of etiquette and conduct, you would still behave unattractively at times. Even if you always relentlessly tried to be perfect in all your thoughts and deeds, you would still fall short. Try as we might to be perfect supermen, we are just fallible human beings. Being human, you will at times be hard to love and make mistakes. Does this mean you are unlovable? Absolutely not! In fact, no matter how far down the scale you have gone, no matter how objectionable your conduct, you should never disqualify yourself from being loved. Even when we think ourselves unlovable, there will always be at least One who loves you – God.

> "I have said these things to you, that in me you may have peace. In the world you will have tribulation. But take heart; I have overcome the world."
> – John 16:33

**TODAY, I WILL WALK IN VICTORY.
I WILL SEE ANY FAILURES AS PUTTING
ME ONE STEP CLOSER TO MY SUCCESS.**

**I MAY EXPERIENCE FAILURE
BUT I WILL NOT BE DEFEATED.**

It's said that Ray Kroc, the founder of McDonald's, was turned down for financing hundreds of times. Legend has it that Walt Disney failed to get financial backing for his idea 302 times. Winston Churchill failed his English class several times. Microsoft founder, Bill Gates, dropped out of college. Still, all these men have made significant achievements in their lives. What propelled them to success and victory? Why, after so many failures and setbacks, did they continue to push forward toward their goal? One truth that they adopted that many miss, is the crucial role failure plays in one's journey to success. They understood that the information learned from failing could help them to improve, regroup, restructure, reapply, re-think, and try again. They understood that each "no" merely meant "not now". Each rejection taught them a lesson that they used to move closer to success. They understood that each failure or setback brought them closer to success. People who succeed know that failure and setbacks are unavoidable steps on the way to success.

> "A time to get, and a time to lose;
> a time to keep, and a time
> to cast away."
>
> – Ecclesiastes 3:6

TODAY, I'LL LET GO OF SOMETHING MINOR. I WON'T GIVE MAJOR ATTENTION TO MINOR MATTERS.

Most of the things that come our way daily are small stuff. Stuff like someone forgetting your name, bumping into you without apology, walking through the door you held open for them and not say "thanks," or the receptionist who puts you on hold and seems to forget about you. We can name more of these examples of seemingly small, unpleasant things that happen to us. When we add it all up, most of the things that happen in our lives are the minor stuff. Because these little things are so numerous, the cumulative effect they have on us can be disastrous. It can feel like everyone is disrespectful, or all women of a certain race are rude or all government employees only want to waste your time or everyone is out to get you. If we choose to hold on to every little thing and resent those who do them, eventually we will start to generalize and expect more of the same. We will become overwhelmed by them. Then, by the time something major comes along, we find we lack the capacity we need to handle it well. Today, choose to let things go. Do not make minor matters major.

> "Good sense makes a man slower to anger, and it is his glory to overlook an offense."
> – Proverbs 19:11

TODAY, I WILL NOT ALLOW OTHER PEOPLE'S BEHAVIOR TO RUIN MY DAY.

NO MATTER WHAT, I'M GOING TO TREAT OTHERS THE WAY I WANT THEM TO TREAT ME. TODAY WILL BE A GOOD DAY FOR ME.

Ever held a door for someone and they just walk through without even saying thank you? Ever got on an elevator and some woman starts holding her pocketbook tighter? Ever been kept waiting in an establishment while others who came after you got served before you? We could list a great number of things we experience as men as we journey through our lives. We are inclined to think these *petty slights* happen because of who we are. This is a lie. The real reason they happen is because of who *they* are. It's their behavior. They made the decision to be ill-mannered, judgmental or selfish. They decided to treat you unfairly. Therefore, they are accountable. You can only be responsible for your actions. Let other people be accountable for theirs.

> **"Iron sharpens iron, and one man sharpens another."**
> – Proverbs 27:17

TODAY, LET US REMEMBER THAT WE ARE INFLUENCERS.

LET US LOOK FOR AT LEAST ONE OPPORTUNITY TO INFLUENCE SOMEONE POSITIVELY.

When we hear the term *influencer*, we most likely think of people on social media who can impact the sales of a brand. They may or may not be celebrities. However, they have large enough audiences that others are willing to pay to access. Though we may not have a following on social media, it does not mean we cannot be influencers. We all have the potential to impact people young and old, in small ways and large. We don't have to be famous or get paid for it. Ordinary folks do a lot of influencing. At some point today, there will be an opportunity to influence someone. Someone needs your influence on his or her life. That person could be any age, creed, color, or social status. How will you respond? You are an influencer, influencing one person at a time. Find someone to influence today.

> "if possible, so far as it depends on you, live peaceably with all."
> - Romans 12:18

TODAY, I'LL PURSUE PEACE AND LOOK FOR MY BROTHERS WHO ARE ALSO LOOKING FOR PEACE.

It's sad how quickly some people want to fight and quarrel over the most trivial issue. Far too many men believe they have something to prove. The question is, do you want to live like that — on edge, with confrontation and violence just a word away? A lot of men simply want to live in peace. Those of us who do want peace must avoid those who prefer the path of conflict and aggression. If we want to live in peace, we must get with likeminded brothers who desire to live in peace and harmony with others.

> "A new commandment I give to you,
> that you love one another: just as I have
> loved you, you are also to love one another."
> – John 13:34

TODAY, I WILL SEE AND BELIEVE THAT ANY TIME IS A GOOD TIME FOR LOVE.

I WILL DECIDE TO LOVE.

TODAY I WILL LOVE.

Arguably, we are living in the most divisive and divided era ever. There may be more hostility and hatred in society than has ever been seen before. There is war in the streets and on the battlefield. Peace, love, and goodwill are being squeezed out of our culture and becoming more unpopular. Sometimes it seems like aggression has replaced civility and neighborliness. All this is enough to move our tension level into the red-zone. But we don't have to go there. There is no rule that says you must go in the same negative direction that the world is going in. In fact, there is a huge opportunity in all this, amidst a lot of despair. The opportunity is for us to make love of our fellow man our way of living. It's an opportunity to pursue peace with our brothers and sisters. We are all brothers and sisters.

> "Be kindly affectionate to one another with brotherly love, in honor giving preference to one another."
> – Romans 12:10

TODAY, LET US COMMIT TO REMEMBERING THAT EVERY MAN IS OUR BROTHER.

LET US DEMONSTRATE LOVE, RESPECT, CARE AND UNDERSTANDING FOR EVERYONE WHOSE PATH WE CROSS.

As we go through life, we can choose to see others through the lens of what separates us, or what unites us. We do not all look or sound the same way but we are one human family. The fact that we are of different ethnicities, countries and socio-economic backgrounds does not change this fact. Regardless of these different identities, we are brothers and sisters. We all belong to the same race – the human race. If you can fix your mind to see that every man is your brother and every woman is your sister, the forces that want to divide us will fail. Sadly, many of us fall into the trap of focusing on our differences. The result is discord and discontent among brothers. We become part of the problem rather than part of the solution. The solution is to never lose sight of the fact that we are brothers, regardless of what we may think. Love your brother,

> "A friend loves at all times,
> and a brother is born for a time
> of adversity."
>
> –Proverbs 17:17

TODAY, LET'S LOOK AT HOW WE LOVE.

Many people, when they say they love you, really mean that they love the way you make them feel. They love you until you displease or disappoint them, or fail to meet their expectations. People's love is often based on what they think they can get from the other person. It's a conditional form of affection which arguably, is not love at all. This is love that comes and goes because it's not based on principle, but on emotion. Check your own experience. How many times have people who claim to love you, go on to treat you badly when they get mad at you? How many times have people terminated a relationship with you and act like you never meant anything to them? It's as if their "love" dried up instantly. What about you? Is your love based on conditions? Is it still there, regardless of fickle feelings? Can you still give or extend love even when the relationship has ended, or does that love turn to hate because the person no longer makes you feel good? How do you love? What does your love look like? Think about it.

www.ingramcontent.com/pod-product-compliance
Lightning Source LLC
Chambersburg PA
CBHW050650160426
43194CB00010B/1886